SAGE CONTEMPORARY SOCIAL SCIENCE ISSUES 7

COMPARATIVE POLITICAL SOCIALIZATION

Edited by
Jack Dennis
and
M. Kent Jennings

Ⓢ SAGE PUBLICATIONS *Beverly Hills / London*

PUBLISHER'S NOTE

The material in this publication originally appeared as a special issue of COMPARATIVE POLITICAL STUDIES (Volume 3, Number 2, July 1970). The Publisher would like to acknowledge the assistance of the special issue editors, Jack Dennis and M. Kent Jennings, in making this edition possible.

Copyright © 1970 by Sage Publications, Inc.

All rights reserved. No part of this book may be reproduced or utilized in any form or by any means, electronic or mechanical, including photocopying, recording, or by any information storage and retrieval system, without permission in writing from the publisher.

For information address:

SAGE PUBLICATIONS, INC.
275 South Beverly Drive
Beverly Hills, California 90212

SAGE PUBLICATIONS LTD
St George's House / 44 Hatton Garden
London EC1N 8ER

Printed in the United States of America

International Standard Book Number 0-8039-0336-7

Library of Congress Catalog Card No. 73-93704

FIRST PRINTING (this edition)

CONTENTS

COMPARATIVE POLITICAL SOCIALIZATION
Edited by Jack Dennis—*University of Wisconsin*
M. Kent Jennings—*University of Michigan*

Introduction
    JACK DENNIS
    M. KENT JENNINGS   5

Family Influence and Political Socialization in Japan: *Some Preliminary Findings in Comparative Perspective*
    AKIRA KUBOTA
    ROBERT E. WARD   11

Political Organization and the Politicization of the Poblador
    DANIEL GOLDRICH   47

School Experiences and Political Socialization: *A Study of Tanzanian Secondary School Students*
    KENNETH PREWITT
    GEORGE VON DER MUHLL
    DAVID COURT   75

Individual Rights and the Public Good: *A Cross-National Study of Adolescents*
    JUDITH GALLATIN
    JOSEPH ADELSON   98

Preadult Development of Political Party Identification in Western Democracies
    JACK DENNIS
    DONALD J. McCRONE   115

INTRODUCTION

Political socialization emerged as a formal arena of inquiry in the late 1950's, and in the space of a decade, became a leading specialization in the discipline of political science. Some appreciation of this phenomenal growth may be obtained by comparing the fourth and fifth editions of the *Biographical Directory* of the American Political Science Association. In the former, published in 1961, political socialization is not even listed as a field. In the edition published in 1968, no less than 767 members of the Association laid claim to the area. So great was the gain that the listings compared favorably with those in many of the time-honored specialties.

Beginning initially with work in the United States, research in the area has more recently spread to other climes. It is not without significance that the rise of interest in political socialization has roughly paralleled the explosive growth in empirically based studies of comparative politics. Indeed, one of the attractions of the new field is its utility in helping to account for similarities and contrasts across political systems. Quite clearly both the theoretical advances in comparative politics and the methodological advances in data collection and analysis have abetted the incorporation of political socialization into the fabric of cross-polity analysis.

The five selections contained in this volume are indicative of the kind of thinking and inquiries now underway in a large number of countries. We think that each of them offers something in the way of theoretical, substantive, or methodological contributions which will serve the cause of those interested in comparative politics and political socialization. Rather than summarize the contents of each article, we will, in brief fashion, set each one within the context of what we believe to be some major concern or problem of comparative political socialization, and then suggest how the paper relates to the particular topic.

As noted above, the study of political socialization first gained prominence in the United States. It was not long, however, before some well-traveled paths between the United States and Western Europe began carrying the ideas and data generated by scholars from both continents. While the reasons for the intrusion of socialization interests into the study of western comparative politics are not hard to divine, the ultimate limitations of such a geographical confinement are severe. To make an obvious point, the range of political cultures encompassed by the so-called western democracies leaves out scores undergoing relatively recent emergence from colonial regimes and others recovering from such traumas as defeat in international war and the ravages of civil war. One might well argue that one of the prime opportunities for introducing political socialization concepts lies precisely where historical discontinuity looms so large.

In their study of Japan, Akira Kubota and Robert E. Ward turn to advantage the discontinuities of modern Japanese history as they seek out the role of the family as an agent of political socialization. A particularly attractive feature of their work is the juxtaposition of aggregate national trends with intrafamilial patterns of transmission. A fortuitous aspect of their study, occasioned in part by farsightedness at the time of study design, is that fairly direct comparisons can be drawn between their results and those from non-Japanese studies even though their study, per se, is confined to Japan. It should also be noted that whereas most studies of preadults have typically sampled from schools or other youth organizations, Kubota and Ward start from a conventional base of adults and then sample preadults attached to these adults. Although there are some disadvantages to this approach, it offers opportunities for "piggyback" operations which may be especially appropriate in comparative research.

Political socialization is most commonly thought of as dealing with preadults; of the published work and that underway, the great bulk deals with children and adolescents. Practitioners in this area are, of course, not unlike students of other forms of socialization. The guiding assumption is that what is learned early is most important. While not gainsaying the general applicability of this theorem, there are at least three reasons for looking beyond the preadult years, and they may be briefly stated. First, the preadult years by no means exhaust the possible range of behaviors and values of political significance even in stable societies; in fact for political socialization much of what is learned in the preadult years is simply an imperfect analogy of what may follow. Second, dramatic and sometimes traumatic system-level changes radically alter the sets of beliefs and behavioral predispositions which the individual brings with him into adulthood; these events are most evident in revolutionary and rapidly changing states. Third, even in the absence of vast, system level changes, individuals find themselves in varying states of reinforcement and undermining of prior socialization; thus, the later life effects of early socialization need to be examined under varying situations.

Daniel Goldrich provides a vivid example of adult level political socialization in his account of squatter settlements in Lima, Peru, and Santiago, Chile. As Goldrich himself acknowledges, the materials he has are not ideal for displaying adult socialization. Yet they are perhaps as suitable as one can find, given the research environment of these and similarly situated instances of intense political confrontation, plus limited accessibility. An especially fascinating aspect of his study is the role of political parties. Whereas most political socialization research dealing with parties fixes on questions of differential preferences and of party attachments as indicators of stability and legitimacy, Goldrich shows how party organizations can foster the acquisition of political resources and the learning of political skills.

One of the more frequent questions asked in discussions of political socialization centers on the role of various socializing agents. Such issues as the complementarity of agents, the sequence and timing of exposure, and the ratios of success to failure are raised. While these are important topics in relatively stable systems, they acquire particular significance in the context of transitional and revolutionary societies. In the measure that the society hopes to create a new political form (postwar China, for example), the upcoming generation needs to be socialized into the new modes of thoughts and behaviors. Thus the configuration of socializing agents assumes crucial proportions.

An example of the place of agents in developing societies occurs in the paper on Tanzanian youth by Kenneth Prewitt, George Von der Muhll, and David Court. In tackling the thorny question of the net impact of differing school succession experiences, they raise the issue of whether age, as such, is a legitimate variable to use in socialization studies. At first glance the answer might seem obviously positive, but they argue to the contrary. Of more general concern, however, are the consequences of various patterns of schooling and how these may be linked to the evolving structure of Tanzanian politics. Although the authors deal with only one country with distinct subcultures, their strategy also seems highly appropriate for truly cross-cultural research.

While much lip service has been paid to the virtues of a psychological-developmental approach to political socialization, few political scientists have approached the subject in this vein. This is no doubt due, in part, to the discipline's relative unfamiliarity with the concepts and findings in the area. Another apparent reason is the fear among many political scientists that such an approach would take them too far from central concerns: skittishness stems from the belief that absorption with developmental psychology will lead the political scientist away from politics. For the most part, then, political scientists seem content to borrow from the developmental psychologists as necessary.

What happens when developmental psychologists themselves turn to the substantive area of political socialization? Few have, but Joseph Adelson and his associates represent conspicuous exceptions. Beginning with an initial base in the United States, they have moved on to the cross-national scene. Their work is intriguing on at least two counts. First, they take up rather global orientations much in the mold of students of moral development. These are topics of a somewhat broader and more diffuse nature than those typically pursued by political scientists. Thus, the psychologists are interested in such concerns as the child's changing sense of community and his notions of law and the legal order. In this issue, Judith Gallatin and Joseph Adelson approach the question of the public good. A second point is that they are not particularly constrained in their theorizing by the absence of large, systematic samples. While the need for the latter is obvious for many purposes, the utility, perhaps the necessity, of intensive work with small numbers in applying developmental psychology to political socialization is apparent. We might note in passing that Gallatin and Adelson tend to stay within the confines of their own discipline in the interpretations and applications of their findings.

A persistent concern of political socialization inquiry in the past decade has been to illuminate the patterns of development of political party identification. Impetus for this special interest has come from a number of sources, but two stand out. One is the compilation of earlier research findings by Hyman in which party preference figured as a benchmark orientation for measuring the influence of family and other agents of socialization.

The other major source was the voting studies, especially those carried out by the University of Michigan's Survey Research Center. The latter demonstrate the importance of partisan orientation both for the individual elector and for the political system. At the voter level, party identification serves to structure the assimilation of new political information—particularly about new candidates and issues. Thus, party identification is important both for the citizen's interpretation of politics and for his voting behavior. On the system level, the distribution of aggregate preferences sets the basic terms within which particular elections are held. In addition, collective extent of partisan allegiance can be taken as an indicator of relative support for the party system as an institution.

The latter aspect of partisan orientation provides the background for the research reported by Jack Dennis and Donald McCrone. They follow a general line of analysis in which party-system stability is linked to patterns of preadult political learning of party identification. In presenting interview data from a number of western nations, including France, Italy, Germany, and Britain, they attempt to trace the relative prospects for stability and change to patterns of early learning. They focus in particular upon age development of partisan self-images prior to voting age and upon the extent of agreement between parents and their progeny at the child's different ages.

What their research demonstrates implicitly is that scholarship has still a considerable distance to go even in an area of empirical analysis of attitude formation where much work has already been done. Our knowledge is remarkably incomplete when we consider that party identification is possibly the most frequently researched orientation both in voting and in political socialization studies. But as we move beyond the United States, knowledge of the evolution of individual preference and the circumstances of partisan transmission across generations remains even today both crude and fragmentary. As adumbrated by Dennis and McCrone, the future possibilities for more dynamic, cross-cultural analyses of developmental patterns of partisan loyalties are virtually unlimited.

In general, then, this special issue takes the reader into hitherto unexplored territory. That there can be this freshness is not surprising given the lightness of past treatment of comparative political socialization phenomena. What little non-American evidence has been generated over the last decade has too often focused narrowly upon a single system and its peculiarities, rather than giving genuine cross-national comparison. We hope that these five reports of empirical findings will stimulate new comparative inquiry, both in developed and developing nations.

FAMILY INFLUENCE AND POLITICAL SOCIALIZATION IN JAPAN

Some Preliminary Findings in Comparative Perspective

AKIRA KUBOTA and ROBERT E. WARD

AKIRA KUBOTA is Research Associate at the Survey Research Center of the University of Michigan. His fields of concentration include politics in East Asia and voting behavior. ROBERT E. WARD is Professor of Political Science at the University of Michigan. He is the author of several books and numerous articles in the fields of comparative politics and political development. He is presently working with Dr. Kubota on a study of political attitudes and behavior in present-day Japan and is also doing a study of planned political change.

For some time it was generally held by American social scientists that in the United States the family was normally the single most important agency of political socialization where children are concerned, and that many political attitudes and values tended to be transmitted from one generation to another via the medium of the family (Hyman, 1959: 69; Elkin, 1960: 46; Davies, 1965). Recent research has expanded and refined our knowledge in political socialization and has questioned this view of family influence as either too simplistic or misleading an explanation of the causality involved (Hess and Torney, 1965: 193, 200; Hess and Torney, 1967: 97-101; Dawson and Prewitt, 1969: 105-108; Jennings and Niemi, 1968: 169-184). Despite such reassessments, however, the weight of the currently available evidence still favors the view that in the United States the family, if not predominant, is still regarded as one of the more important agencies of political socialization and that this is particularly

---

AUTHORS' NOTE: *This is a revised version of a paper delivered at the annual meeting of the American Political Science Association in New York in September, 1969. The research on which this article is based was made possible by financial support from the National Science Foundation, the Carnegie Corporation of New York, and the Ford Foundation. The survey data used were gathered by Yoron Kagaku Kyokai of Tokyo, in accordance with a research design developed by the*

true with respect to such seminal traits as party identification on the part of the child (Jennings and Niemi, 1968).

Given a somewhat shifting point of view in this respect on the local scene, it is of special interest and importance to look abroad at the results of research relating to the process of political socialization in other modern political systems to see if they confirm or disaffirm our current hypotheses. The present article represents a preliminary and somewhat tentative effort to do so with respect to contemporary Japanese experience in this field.

Political socialization has not been a popular subject of study among Japanese social scientists. The relevant literature is scant and tends to be ephemeral and semipopular in quality. If there has been any single focus that stands out, it has probably been on shifts that are alleged to have been taking place in the electoral behavior of young voters and the probable effects of these on the future of particular political parties. Also, since the survey approach is expensive and still relatively little used by Japanese social scientists, the evidential basis for those viewpoints that have been expressed is apt to be impressionistic and episodic.

Despite such shortcomings there has grown up on the basis of both indigenous and foreign commentary a sort of lore about the process of political socialization in Japan. It is notable that this does not usually correspond to the popular stereotypes of Japan widely held abroad. Many might be tempted to see in modern Japan a society where the centrality of the family's role is historically reinforced by centuries of Confucian tradition, and, until recently, by the mythology of a family-centered state and the sociopolitical circumstances of a preponderantly agrarian culture as well. The ready conclusion would be that the role of the family as an agent of political socialization is, if anything, more dominant and salient than in a more atomized American society.

While continuity in this sense is an important attribute of Japanese culture, it is, however, possible to view the society from another

---

authors. *The authors wish to acknowledge their indebtedness to the Center for Japanese Studies and the Survey Research Center of the University of Michigan and to Philip E. Converse, Donald E. Stokes, and Suzuki Tatsuzo for assisting them in designing and administering the study and in analyzing the data subsequently gathered. M. Kent Jennings has generously made available some of his published and unpublished data on political socialization in the United States, while Kenneth P. Langton and Paul Beck have been kind enough to discuss and criticize certain of our findings. Tables and figures presented in this article were prepared in the first instance by our research assistants, Suzuki Toshiko and Harlan Himel. Robert E. Ward would also like to express his gratitude to the Center for Advanced Study in the Behavioral Sciences, where his share of the article was written.*

perspective—that of change. This leads to the observation that since the Meiji Restoration of 1868, Japan has been more or less constantly involved in a process of society-wide change that has certainly been revolutionary in effect, if not in format. Defeat in World War II and its aftermath, the Allied Occupation, with its attempts to remake the society along more democratic and western lines, is simply the latest in a series of wrenching episodes that stretch back for a least a hundred years. Seen from this viewpoint, rapid and disturbing changes in the economic, social, and political spheres have been more or less normal in modern Japan. They have, inevitably, exacted a price in terms of intergenerational harmony. Older generations in Japan have been complaining for a century about a lack of rapport with, and influence over, their children. The term "generation gap" was widely used in Japan long before it became popular in the United States (Lifton, 1962). It is this aspect of the society on which students of political socialization have elected to concentrate, with the result that the influence of the family as an agent of political socialization tends normally to be discounted (see, for example, Kuroda, 1965).

Contemporary Japanese culture affords, however, theoretical grounds for looking at the process of political socialization in two quite different—indeed, almost polarized—ways: one of which emphasizes continuity and the primacy of the family as a socializing agent, while the other focuses on change, discontinuity, and the salience of such nonfamilial agencies of socialization as peer groups, life cycle effects, education, and the mass media. Neither hypothesis need completely exclude the other; overlays and sectoral differences in causality are possible. Despite this, the resultant confrontation is challenging in theoretical terms and of obvious comparative importance in the attempts of social scientists to comprehend the process of political socialization in modern societies in general. The issues are complex; anything approximating a satisfactory solution will require investigation in depth and over a substantial period of time. All that the present paper hopes to do is to provide—in a national case marked so far by a paucity of "hard" data—a few leads and guidelines derived from a national public opinion survey that the authors recently conducted in Japan.

Our data are based on a larger study that we conducted in connection with the general election of members of the lower house of Japan's National Diet or parliament, held on January 29, 1967. Three surveys were involved, two mass and one elite. The two mass surveys were conducted just before and just after the election. They were based on a single stratified national probability sample (n = 2,371 individuals) of the Japanese population, aged fifteen and above, drawn from 50 of the 123 election districts that returned candidates to the lower house. The elite survey was carried out after the election and involved a sample of 315 candidates running for parliamentary office from the same fifty election districts. The response rate on the preelection mass survey was 81%, that on the postelection mass survey, 76%, while the figure for the elite survey reached 90%.

The findings reported here are based primarily on a sample of 177 child-parent pairs included within the sample. They are augmented where appropriate by information from the total sample. Several other characteristics of the data require explanation. First, although they are derived from a nationwide sample so that their means are unbiased estimates of true national means, it should be clear that the sampling errors involved are quite large in comparison with those of a standard national cross-section sample of 1,500 or more respondents. Second, the sampling errors of age-related variables are considerably reduced since age was one of the variables about which our sample was stratified. This should increase the potency of the data in analyzing problems related to generational continuity or discontinuity. Finally, the sample was specifically designed with a view toward maximizing the quality of our measurement of family influence. We attempted to do this by selecting our child-parent pairs from the same family. This was done by first drawing a sample of adults; i.e., twenty years of age and above (who were also electors; twenty is the legal voting age in Japan) and by examining to see if they had children aged fifteen through nineteen. If they did, we then drew a sample of those in this age bracket on a probability basis. The chief purpose of this was to enable us to measure family influence on the basis of both direct or observed data and indirect or perceived data; both children and parents could be questioned directly about their own attitudes and behavior, as well as about their perceptions of the other's views and actions. The results of the two approaches are by no means identical.

There are obvious limitations to the methodology of this sort of investigation. It is for this reason that we referred to the study earlier as preliminary and tentative; it is a pilot study of the sort that normally precedes a large-scale standard study. We do hope, however, that in a field marked largely by speculation, these findings may serve to suggest approaches and hypotheses for further field investigation.

THEORETICAL SETTING

Much of the argumentation for the popular thesis that the family is not a particularly effective agency of political socialization in contemporary Japan derives from rather generally held beliefs about the generation gap. This is viewed as being widespread and basic. One conclusion is that one must look primarily to agencies of political socialization other than the family to explain the consequent differences in generational attitudes and behavior. There is some evidence that appears to argue in favor of such a conclusion.

One of the most striking pieces of evidence of this sort is provided by the way in which party identification in Japan varies with age. The common claim is that younger generations tend to be more progressive (*shimpoteki*), and older generations conservative (*hoshuteki*) in their party identifications. The principal objects of the identifications involved are usually the Japan Socialist Party (JSP) for the progressives and the Liberal Democratic Party (LDP) for the conservatives. Ignoring the semantic appropriateness of the labels, our data set forth in Figure 1 support such a view subject to the qualification that this should not be taken to mean that most younger voters are progressive in their party identifications. It is simply that they are more apt to display such a tendency than their seniors.[1] It is obvious, however, that age is positively correlated with identification with Japan's major conservative party, the LDP, and negatively correlated with identification with the largest socialist party, the JSP. The tendency is particularly marked from the late thirties. Data of this sort suggest that in many Japanese households there is virtually no transmission of party identification from one generation to another.

Once one has begun along lines such as this to discount the role of the family as a socializing agent, reference to alternative and putatively more effective agents lends added support. There is no doubt that in Japan as in other modern societies the socializing influence of peer groups, the educational system, and the mass media are factors of some significance. Most of these seem to display a fairly marked bias toward progressive attitudes and values, and thus may be viewed as reinforcing the hypothesis that Japanese youth are moving away from the political views of their parents.

These are what might be termed microforces affecting the process of political socialization. Beyond these lies an array of macroforces which may also play a determining role. They consist of the entire spectrum of social, economic and political changes that have cumulated over the last

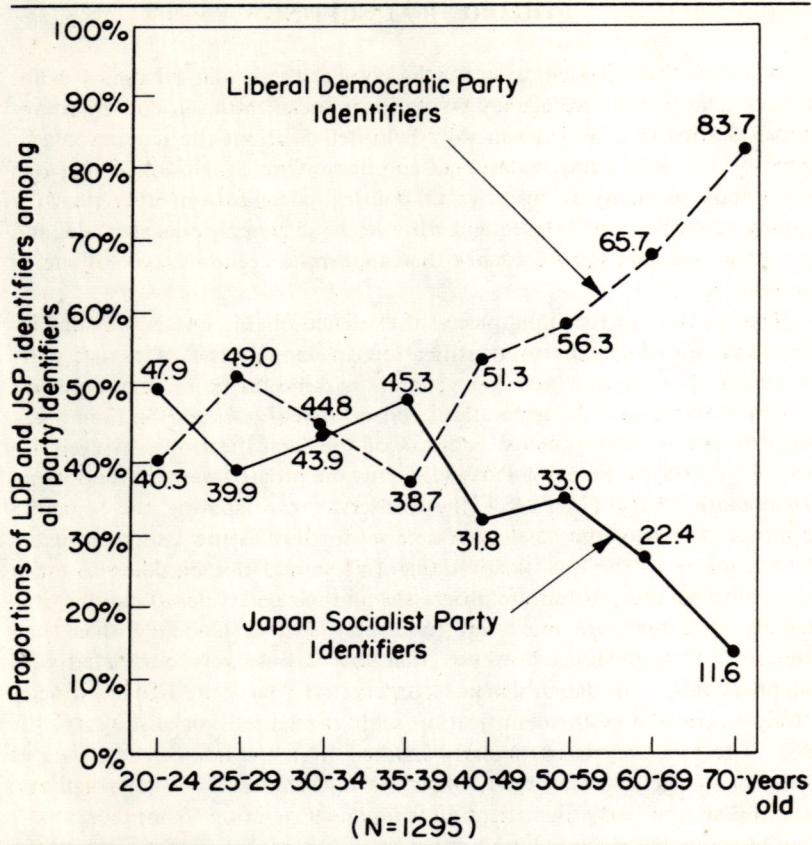

Figure 1. PARTY IDENTIFICATION AND AGE

century. The record is an impressive one. No nation starting from a nonwestern base has ever achieved the modern condition in so short a period of time as Japan. The process of change involved has been massive, continuous and, for many, deeply disturbing. Many of the most seminal innovations have taken place since the end of World War II and thus have had a direct effect upon today's youth and their parents.

The educational system has been fundamentally revised along more individualistic and democratic lines. There has been a sweeping reform in the ownership of agricultural land that has reduced the traditionally high rate of rural tenancy to a nominal figure and vastly improved the circumstances of the remaining tenants. The unionization and politicization of labor has become normal rather than exceptional. The national economy has expanded and advanced in every direction, and from postwar circumstances characterized by devastation and stagnation, has recently become the third most potent and productive in the world, surpassing West Germany and Great Britain. As a consequence, standards of living and levels of expectation have increased enormously for almost the entire population over prewar highs, and the people of Japan have for the first time been brought face to face with that peculiar problem of advanced industrial societies—what they call the "*rejā* [leisure] boom," or the problem of how to deal with unprecedented amounts of free time in an affluent society. Communication and transportation systems have changed accordingly and any effective degree of social or geographical isolation has become an artifact of the past. Politically the country has been shifted from the basically oligarchic and authoritarian structure of the Meiji Constitution to the remarkably free, open, and democratic institutions of the Constitution of 1947.

This is an impressive record of change for a twenty-five-year period in the history of any country, and given the contrasts between pre- and postwar conditions and the widely variant experiences of the different age cohorts involved, it is certainly a set of circumstances calculated to maximize all possible aspects of the generation gap and accordingly reduce the conservative influence of the family as a socializing agency.

One can muster in this manner a number of arguments to demonstrate that in Japan, macroforces have been combining with microforces to enhance the generation gap and diminish familial influence. Some might be tempted to go beyond this and claim that such a circumstance is normal for rapidly modernizing or changing societies (Kuroda, 1965: 328). The thesis is attractive, but it is not without difficulties. One such difficulty derives from the fact that a rapid rate of change at the macrolevel does not necessarily lead to a comparable rate of change at the microlevel, especially where individual attitudes and behavior are concerned. While there is probably a long-run tendency for the two to converge, in the short run, attitudes and behavior are apt to remain much more stable than one would expect, given the scope of macrochanges in the environment. In Japan, for example, the distribution of partisan support and the distribution of political power have remained remarkably stable over the postwar period (Nishihira, 1963: 93-136). There have been no changes at this level that correspond in scale or importance to the truly remarkable changes noted earlier in the economy or society at large.

If such a discrepancy exists between the thrust of socializing forces operating at the societal macrolevel and actual patterns of attitudes and behavior at the individual level, it suggests the action of intervening causes and thus redirects our attention to forces operating at the microlevel—in the present case, specifically to the family. The socializing influence of the family tends to be profound and tends to be conservative. It normally attempts to transmit to the next generation its own values and standards of the moment (Dawson and Prewitt, 1969: 124-125; Vogel, 1967). It is for this reason that states dedicated to programs of drastic and rapid social change, such as the Peoples Republic of China, have so often found it necessary to try to alter the structure and influence of the family. Beyond this, however, there are at least two other reasons for emphasizing the importance of the family as an agent of socialization.[2] One is timing, and the other, magnitude of exposure. Greenstein (1965: 80) and others (Spiro, 1955: 1249) claim that the earlier the exposure to given attitudes and values, the greater their impact. Although there may be more than a single phase to early political learning and the processes involved may be even more complicated than we now realize, there is no question that the family normally plays a dominant role in the child's early life (Greenstein, 1965: 55-84; Elkin, 1960: 46-47).

Sheer magnitude of exposure is another reason. For reasons of physical proximity alone, children are usually most intensively and comprehensively exposed to the families into which they are born (Dawson and Prewitt, 1969: 107-108). This degree of exposure seems well calculated to affect at least the child's earlier political perceptions and attitudes. As the child grows older, of course, this monolithic influence of the family is progressively diluted by competing agencies such as peer groups, schools, the mass media, work groups, and so forth, and these tend to become relatively more salient sources of socializing pressures.

If we then juxtapose in the Japanese case the two levels of socializing influences that we have been discussing—the macrolevel and the microlevel—an interesting situation results. Approaching the problem of political socialization from the macrolevel, we should be inclined to hypothesize that the changes involved have been severely restrictive of the effectiveness of parents as agents of political socialization. Viewing it from the microlevel, however, we find reasons to affirm the existence of an appreciable degree of parental influence over the socialization process. Recognizing that there is probably some validity to both approaches leads us to speculate that the macro- and microforces probably interact on individuals and to some extent cancel each other out. This in turn leads to the further speculation that one will in fact be able to detect family influence on the political socialization process, but that this will be moderate in degree. What do the survey data show in this respect?

EVIDENCE

The findings of both the first and second wave of the mass survey clearly confirm the existence of a moderate degree of correspondence between parent's party identification and that of his or her child. Table 1, reflecting the results of the first or preelection wave of the survey, shows a tau-b correlation of .39. Table 2, reflecting the results of the second or

TABLE 1
CHILD-PARENT PAIRS AND PARTY IDENTIFICATION
(FIRST WAVE)
(in percentages)

		Child's Party Identification						
		LDP[a]	CGP	DSP	JSP	JCP	Total %	n
Parent's Party Identification	LDP	67.1	2.6	5.2	25.1	0.0	100.0	(41)
	CGP	33.3	50.0	0.0	16.7	0.0	100.0	(6)
	DSP	100.0	0.0	0.0	0.0	0.0	100.0	(3)
	JSP	19.2	0.0	7.7	73.1	0.0	100.0	(14)
	JCP	0.0	0.0	0.0	0.0	100.0	100.0	(2)
tau-b = .39	Total	53.4	6.4	4.8	32.2	3.2	100.0	(66)

a. There are five major political parties in Japan at the present moment. The LDP (Liberal Democratic Party) is a successor of the two prewar major conservative Parties. It is, as made clear in Table 1, the largest party in Japan today. The JSP (Japan Socialist Party), the second-largest party, began occupying seats in the Diet in the 1930s and has been a major party since 1945. The DSP (Democratic Socialist Party) is an offshoot of the JSP, but is more conservative and a smaller party. The JCP (Japan Communist Party) is very small, and it has generally held less than a half-dozen seats in the lower house since World War II. The CGP (Clean Government Party) is a religious party and its issue position is not too different from that of the DSP. The CGP is similar in size to the DSP.
   The particular version of ordering of these five parties used in Table 1 and subsequent tables in this article was determined on the basis of two types of analysis. One is that of evaluating the issue position of each of the parties more or less subjectively as was sketched out in the preceding paragraph and arranging these parties accordingly along the liberal-conservative dimension. The kind of operation involved and the type of result arrived at by this method are not too different from those generally used by many Japanese political commentators. Another type of analysis is that of multidimensional scaling of party data gathered in this study. The specific method used was the Shepard-Kruskal version of the nonmetric multidimensional-scaling algorithm, and our input data were processed in the way that French data were processed by Philip E. Converse (1966). In both of these analyses we arrived at the same ordering of the five major Japanese political parties.

TABLE 2
CHILD-PARENT PAIRS AND PARTY IDENTIFICATION
(SECOND WAVE)
(in percentages)

		Child's Party Identification						
		LDP	CGP	DSP	JSP	JCP	Total %	n
Parent's Party Identification	LDP	68.5	2.5	2.5	26.5	0.0	100.0	(40)
	CGP	0.0	66.7	0.0	33.3	0.0	100.0	(3)
	DSP	100.0	0.0	0.0	0.0	0.0	100.0	(2)
	JSP	38.5	0.0	15.4	46.2	0.0	100.0	(14)
	JCP	0.0	0.0	0.0	25.0	75.0	100.0	(4)
tau-b = .38	Total	55.0	5.0	5.0	30.0	5.0	100.0	(63)

postelection wave, shows a tau-b correlation of .38. These rule out either an extremely strong relationship between the two variables or, at the other extreme, a significant degree of independence of one variable from the other, and lead one back to the middle-ground hypothesis that there is a moderate degree of overall association between the variables under examination. In other words, the data furnish some basis for belief that a child's party identification may to some extent be related to that of his parents, and that party identification is in a significant number of cases transmitted from parents to children in Japanese households.

Two further factors add to the probability of this hypothesis. First, there is very little change in the correlation coefficient from one wave of the survey to the other. Given a highly visible and strenuously competitive national political campaign, it is to be expected that some changes in partisan attitudes and identifications will take place over the campaign period. However, insofar as the correlation involved reflects an effective process of generational transmission of party identification, one would expect the coefficient to remain reasonably stable when measured at two such intervals. This is the present case. The difference between the two scores is remarkably small.[3]

Second, when respondents below voting age (from fifteen through nineteen) were queried as to their memory of the party with which they had first identified as children (rather than their current party identifications) and the answers were correlated with their parent's party identifications, we obtained tau-b scores of .45 for the first wave, and .48 for the second wave.[4] While similar to the coefficients in Tables 1 and 2, they are, of course, somewhat higher. This may certainly be due in part to distortion attendant upon the recall process involved.[5] It also seems probable to us that it is in a great measure related to the process whereby party identifications emerge during early childhood and develop as children grow up.[6] This upward shift in the value of the coefficients is consistent with the interpretation that the family is most effective as an agent of political socialization during the child's younger years and that as the child matures and is progressively exposed to more and competitive socializing agencies, he tends in many cases to move away from the sphere of family influence in this and other respects. This is a dynamic aspect of the process of political socialization that needs more systematic investigation, but in any event the above interpretation does significantly reduce the probability that the degree of intergenerational agreement in party identification described above is merely accidental.

Before turning to a more comparative dimension of the significance of the relationship developed in Tables 1 and 2, it is worth commenting briefly on the political implications of these data. The differences by party in the relative effectiveness of parents in transmitting their own party identifications to their children are intriguing. Due to sizeable variations in the first- and second-wave responses, they are also difficult to interpret and subject to very large margins of error. They do suggest, however, that parents of communist persuasion are the most effective socializers of their children in this respect, and surprisingly, they may be followed by parents favoring the LDP. The relative consistency of the LDP responses across the two waves is interesting in this respect. So too are the quite consistent totals for the percentages of the fifteen- through nineteen-year-old bracket being identified with each of the five parties, and particularly the ranges of 53.4-55.0% for the LDP, and 32.2-30.0% for the JSP. Both ranges exceed the percentage of the total vote polled by the LDP (48.8%) and the JSP (27.9%) in the 1967 general election, but, to the degree that they are reliable, this showing of the partisan inclinations of the upcoming cohorts of new voters suggests a far more serious problem for the Socialists than for the Liberal Democrats. The Japan Socialist Party has tended to rely heavily on its appeal to the youth vote (see Figure 1).[7]

Comparatively speaking, party identification has been a focal point in the American study of electoral behavior. Voting studies, especially those emerging from the University of Michigan's Survey Research Center, have persistently pointed to important relationships between party identification and various forms of electoral behavior (Campbell et al., 1960; Campbell et al., 1966). This emphasis on party identification has also been carried over to studies of political socialization and has emerged as one of its main areas of investigation. This is due in part to the fact that voting behavior cannot be fully understood without studying the process of political socialization. But also involved is the fact that in studies of political socialization, party identification has been found to exhibit some unusual characteristics. It seems to be an area in which the largest degree of positive generational transmission takes place (Jennings and Niemi, 1968: 172-174; Hyman, 1959: 70-72).

It should also be pointed out, however, that recent research indicates that the degree to which parents in the United States pass on their party identifications to their children is not as great as it was once thought to be. A major study by Jennings and Niemi (1968: 172-173), for example, found a tau-b correlation of .47. Niemi (1967: 97-138, 178-187) has separately explored this problem, but it is clear that the higher correlations found in earlier studies at least partly result from the practice of substituting perceived data for observed data, and that in such cases the respondent's tendency to reduce cognitive dissonance is apt to distort the resultant statistics. If this difficulty is avoided through reliance only on directly measured data, the lower levels of correlation found by the Jennings-Niemi study and the present one may prove to be the more accurate.

The correlation coefficients of .39 and .38 for the two waves of this study are lower than but not markedly different from the Jennings-Niemi figure of .47. This is interesting both in view of the higher correlations normally assigned in the United States by earlier studies, and the rather widely held view described earlier that in Japan the degree of correlation is very low. Our figures linked to those of Jennings and Niemi suggest that actually there is not a great deal of difference in the extent to which parents in the two societies transmit their party identifications to their children. If so, this is a comparative finding of considerable potential importance, if it can be confirmed by more extensive and specifically focused research. At this point, however, it seems appropriate simply to note the correspondence of findings and to refrain from premature speculations as to the degrees of similarity that may obtain in so complex a process as political socialization in two societies of such disparate cultural and political heritages.

Still, if one presses this line of inquiry as far as our data permit and seeks other points that argue in favor of the hypothesis that the processes of political socialization are in important respects similar in Japan and the United States, some evidence is available. Figure 2 sets forth in scaled and comparative fashion a group of correlation coefficients between children's and parents' political attitudes and attributes in Japan and the United

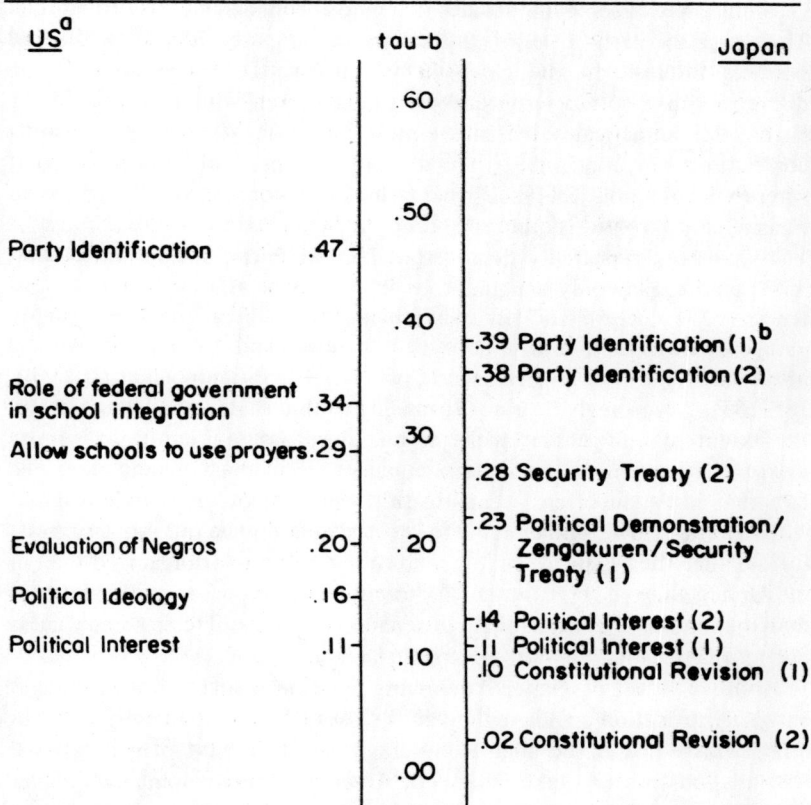

a. From Jennings and Niemi, 1968a: 169-184 and unpublished statistics supplied by Jennings.
b. Numbers in the parentheses represent the waves of the survey.

Figure 2. GENERATIONAL AGREEMENT OF POLITICAL ATTITUDES: JAPAN AND THE UNITED STATES

States. Some items on the scale are, of course, more directly and meaningfully comparable than others; e.g., party identification and, perhaps, political interest. The rest, with the exception of political ideology, represent degrees of agreement between parents' and children's responses to questions calculated to elicit information about attitudes on currently salient issues of major political importance. They, of course, differ between the two countries.

Similarities of some importance do emerge from an analysis of Figure 2. This is particularly true of the categories of party identification and political interest. In the case of the former, the values are not too discrepant in absolute terms and are similar in rank order as well. In the latter, the numerical values are almost identical. Where the remaining correlations are concerned, they demonstrate primarily the thesis that where specific political issue orientations are concerned, the degree of transmission involved is quite small in both Japan and the United States.

It has been repeatedly demonstrated in American voting studies that issues tend to play only marginal roles in campaigns, that issue orientations tend to be less central and less stable than other political attitudes, notably party identification, and that issue attitudes tend to be only weakly interrelated and poorly organized (Converse, 1964; Campbell et al., 1960: 188-265). Accordingly, it is not surprising to find that in the United States the extent of intergenerational transmission of issue orientations is quite meager. This seems to be at least equally true in the Japanese case. The fact that in Japan often twenty to thirty percent of the sample respond with "don't know" (*wakaranai*) to most standard issue questions suggests further that their issue-attitude structure is even more disorganized than in the United States.[8] It is interesting to note with respect to both countries that the extent of generational consonance tends to increase somewhat as one moves from less to more controversial issues.

Another aspect of Figure 2 deserving mention is that in both countries party identification stands highest in the list of correlation coefficients. In other words this is the area where the greatest amount of generational transmission seems to take place. The American figure is somewhat higher than its Japanese couterpart, and the gap that separates it from the next-highest coefficient on the scale is wider. The Japanese list is not as complete as the American in these respects. In our survey we did find a few attitudes that scaled higher than those for party identification. These were of two sorts. The first includes coefficients that fluctuated wildly and inexplicably from the first to the second wave, or which were measured in only one of the two waves.[9] They were viewed as unstable or uncertain and are excluded from Figure 2. The second excluded category consists of coefficients concerning party-related attitudes which vary greatly from party to party in the Japanese multiparty system.[10] These last, however, tend to support the view that it is in the area of party identification that one finds the largest amount of generational transmission of political attitudes.

The question naturally arises as to why this should be so. Campbell and his associates (Campbell et al., 1960: 42-88) present an extended account of the perception of parties, candidates, and issues in the American case, but it is essentially due to the fact that political parties are both more concrete and more salient than most other political objects. So far as the mass public is concerned, parties and personalities are far more visible than issues, and since personalities come and go, parties tend to acquire a superior historical dimension and continuity that makes them one of the most important variables in the cognitive processes of the public. By and large we believe this to be the case in Japan, although with the qualification that, since the history of Japanese political parties is much briefer than that of American or British parties, and since the party scene in Japan has been notably less stable, we do not expect Japanese party identifications or attitudes to be as well or deeply developed.[11] Still, political competition is keen in Japan and public interest high, especially at election times.

There are other arguments derived from theorizing about the American experience that also seem applicable to Japan in this connection. Greenstein (1965: 71-75, 80) holds, for example, that party identification is transmitted from parent to child at a very early stage of political socialization, and that the development of a party orientation thus clearly precedes those of candidate or issue orientations. He goes on to argue that the younger the child is, the more uncritical and receptive he is apt to be toward values or attitudes that his parents display either purposefully or inadvertently. He concludes that party identification is a field in which the greatest degree of such transmission is apt to take place. Greenstein also reinforces this thesis with a concept borrowed from acculturation studies, namely, those attitudes that are learned earliest are likely to be the most internalized, and those learned later, more superficial and unstable.

We would like at this point to return to our former hypothesis about the interaction of macroforces and microforces in the process of political socialization in Japan. It will be recalled that the effect of the macroforces (major trends of economic, social, and political change over time) was to diminish the intergenerational transmission of political attitudes, while the effect of the microforces, in this case the family, was to enhance the degree of generational continuity. The question is, How does the interaction of macro- and microforces take place? Are there intervening sociological or attitudinal variables that significantly affect the process of generational transmission? If so, which are apt to be more significant at the individual level?

Table 3 has been prepared in an attempt to shed some light on these questions. It is based upon a division of our sample of parent-child pairs into two groups, one of which has been subjected to particular experiences that are often, albeit somewhat arbitrarily, regarded as change-oriented, such as urban as opposed to rural residence, union membership as opposed to nonunion status, high social class, income, or degree of parental education versus their low equivalents, and so on; the other group is composed of those sharing the reciprocal experiences to the above that are here regarded as being oriented toward continuity. These two groups have then been examined in terms of the degree to which the status designated as change-oriented and that designated as continuity-oriented has produced agreement between the parent's and the child's party identifications in order to determine if in fact the variable concerned seems to have enhanced or diminished generational continuity in this respect. The correlation coefficients that result should be conservatively interpreted, however, because of the small size of the sample as a whole and the limited number of cases in each cell. The double column of entries under the rubric codes in Table 3 is explanatory of the categories being used. For example, where the entries opposite population at the top of the table are

TABLE 3
AGREEMENT BETWEEN CHILD'S AND PARENT'S PARTY IDENTIFICATIONS BY DEMOGRAPHIC AND ATTITUDINAL VARIABLES

Control Variables	First Wave Change	First Wave Continuity	Second Wave Change	Second Wave Continuity	Codes	
Population	.23[a]	.60	.29	.50	Large	Small
Administrative level	.36	.49	.34	.46	Urban	Rural
Union membership	.62	.34	.63	.20	Yes	No
Subjective social class	.24	.52	-.02	.50	High	Low
Household income	.52	.36	.43	.32	High	Low
Parent's education	.18	.65	.42	.32	High	Low
Parent's political interest	.36	.53	.45	.23	High	Low
Child's political interest	.55	.20	.42	.32	High	Low
Child's attitudes toward:						
Individual or family	.13	1.00	.16	.89	Indiv.	Family
New or old man	.02	.55	.28	.43	New	Old
Spending or saving	.31	.37	.32	.39	Spend	Save
Youth discipline	.49	.28	.59	.34	Less	More
Respect for parents' view	.41	.32	.37	.24	No	Yes

a. Entries are tau-b coefficients.

concerned, the coefficients .23 under the first wave and .29 under the second are associated with large populations—the coefficients .60 and .50 are associated with small populations.

When we divide our sample in this manner into change-oriented and continuity-oriented contingents, we find considerable variation in the association between parents' and children's party identifications. Urbanization, for example, is generally regarded as a key element in the process of social change. Our results support the view where the generational transmission of party identification is concerned. Whether measured by size of population or by administrative distinctions between urban and rural civil subdivisions, and whether measured by first- or second-wave responses, there is a markedly greater tendency for intergenerational changes of party identification in cities, and for intergenerational continuity in this respect in the countryside.

Where union membership is concerned the results are consistent but would argue an initial error in assigning union status to the change rather than to the continuity group. The coefficients indicate a very marked tendency for the children of union parents to share the party identifications of their parents, compared to a relatively low tendency for such transmission to occur in nonunion families. This is interesting but not really surprising in terms of the fact that our mass survey data as a whole indicate that union membership is one of the most significant variables in predicting both the party identification and the electoral choice of voters in general. Beyond this, however, union membership turns out to be remarkably issue-free. It is not related to stands on most partisan issues.

According to Table 3, subjective social class at first seems to play the anticipated role as an intervening and change-oriented variable, the thesis being in this case that the middle class tends to be more receptive to new information and ideas, and hence more susceptible to change, than does the working class. Yet it is difficult to reconcile the coefficients for social class with those that follow for household income if one grants that higher social class is correlated with higher income. The two sets of coefficients are mutually opposed in this case, and we do not understand why this should be so. The same is true when one uses the level of the parent's education as a critical variable. The results of the second wave reverse those of the first for unknown reasons.

If we compare these findings from our parent-child sample with the results of our mass survey as a whole, it is clear from the latter that these three variables—social class, income, and educational level—are intercorrelated to a significant degree. However, it also emerges that, with the partial exception of educational level, all of them are in the Japanese case either unrelated or only weakly correlated to partisan attitudes or to the change versus continuity issues that were used in the bottom part of Table 3. In comparative terms one expects an intercorrelation of these three variables in any developed society, but the lack of a further relationship between them and other political attitudes and issues in the Japanese case is rather surprising to those familiar with the American and British experiences. It may be that the impact of such demographic variables on partisan attitudes and change versus continuity issues in Japan is different than elsewhere, a point that deserves further investigation.

When we move from demographic to psychological variables, we first find that the level of parental political interest plays an ambiguous role. In the first wave high parental interest is negatively correlated with the degree of generational transmission, but in the second wave that relationship is reversed. When we turn to the level of the child's political interest, however, the pattern is consistent for both waves: higher political interest is associated with a higher degree of generational transmission of party identification, and lower political interest with a lower degree of generational transmission of party identification.

Here, too, it is possible to approach the problem of generational transmission of party identification from either the macro- or the microlevel. At the former one can hypothesize that a high level of major social, economic, and political change in a society is apt to produce a higher level of political interest among youth, and that this higher level of interest conjoined with the presence of major changes in the social environment is apt to produce discordance between the political views and party identifications of children and parents who were exposed to different socializing influences. The comparable hypothesis at the microlevel would be that a high level of political interest among children makes it more probable that the child will be more aware of political cues, and given the timing and intensity of his exposure to his parents and the cues they provide, will be more apt to share their party identification.

Our data provide support for the microlevel hypothesis. Whether we are examining the child's interest in the election, concern with the outcome of the election, or his political interest in general, and whether we are dealing with the results of the first or second wave of the survey, we invariably find a positive relationship between the level of the child's interest and the extent of generational transmission of party identification.[12]

We turn next to the last five variables in Table 3 that deal with the child's attitudes. When we control for specific reference to the way in which the child perceives his relationship to his family, a striking result is obtained.[13] This is a variable that not surprisingly displays a very strong relation to the parent-child consonance of party identification, as Table 3 makes clear. Some aspects of this family-individual or child-family relationship issue are probably more salient in Japan than in the United States or Great Britain. Since the war, there have been critical legal and social changes that have drastically affected the traditional structure of the Japanese family. The predominant view in education and the mass media now is restrictive with respect to the family and supportive of increased individualism. As a consequence, the family itself and its proper role and internal relationships have become something of a political issue in contemporary Japan. Whatever the degree of Japan's peculiarity in this respect, however, it would seem probable from these coefficients that the family does exert an influence on the political socialization of its children and that the extent of generational transmission of party identification is sharply affected by the child's view of his relationship to his family.

The new- or old-man dimension is a variant of the preceding variable.[14] The two dimensions are moderately correlated and are considered to be ideologically interrelated in Japan. Table 3 indicates that a child considering himself a new-type person often deserts his parent's party identification—a child considering himself an old-type person is relatively much more apt to inherit the parent's attitude in this respect. The degree of variation in coefficients is smaller though than in the case of the individual-or-family variable.

A third dimension that is quite important in the life of the average Japanese seems to have little effect on the transmission of party identification. The save-spend issue is a favorite topic of daily conversation among Japanese and also a matter of real national importance.[15] It is closely linked to the system of traditional values that strongly and effectively encourages saving. The savings rate even in the present affluent and consumer-oriented society is among the world's highest. Despite this, it apparently has little relation to the generational transmission of party identification.

The last two variables in Table 3—youth discipline and respect for parents' view—seem to affect the process of generational transmission in a somewhat surprising way.[16] One would normally expect that a child who thinks that today's youth needs more discipline would be more apt to accept his parent's party identification. The coefficients in Table 3 indicate that the opposite is the case; a discipline-oriented youth is more apt to desert his parent's identification in this regard than is a freedom-oriented child. The same is true in the case of respect for parents' view, although in neither case is the extent of the variation in coefficients particularly large.

It is difficult to explain this relationship adequately. It should be noted, however, that questions concerning the generation gap provide the basis for very lively and widespread controversy in Japan and that these matters of youth discipline and respect for parents' views lie close to the heart of the issue. They tend to elicit emotionally charged reactions and are in this sense fairly provocative. On the other hand, the two earlier questions about the family-individual relationship and the new- or old-man dimension are relatively free from this type of difficulty, and our family-individual question may thus be preferable to our parental-view question for the purpose of gathering data dealing with the child's attitudes toward his family or parents. In any event, our data on the two more sensitive questions are considerably different from those on the two other questions and are in fact somewhat negatively correlated.[17]

FATHER VERSUS MOTHER

Another area of major interest with respect to the generational transmission of party identification is the relative roles of the father and the mother in the transmission process. Which is the more influential? There is no question that within the average Japanese household each parent plays a markedly different role (Dore, 1958: chs. 8, 10, 11, 20). This is true with respect to division of labor, parental responsibilities, authority, or even in the area of religion where the role of the father appears to differ from that of the mother in either factual or normative terms. In general, in the Sino-Japanese culture area it is customary for the father to be recognized as the dominant and authoritative figure within the household. Such a status is legitimated by the centuries of Confucian orthodoxy which have only recently been undermined in law. Against such a background it is tempting to assume that the Japanese father plays the predominant role in the political socialization of his children. But is this true in fact? Do Japanese parents have specifically differentiated roles and influences in this sphere? What happens in the case where father and mother are themselves of different partisan persuasions?

When we look beyond Japan we see that ostensibly the male in general plays the leading role in the politics of all modern nations. Again, one is tempted to conclude by extension that fathers do the same in the area of transmitting party identification to their children. Research in the United States, however, does not confirm such a hypothesis. Maccoby, Mathews, and Morton (Maccoby et al., 1954) were among the first to point out the superiority of the mother over the father in this respect in their experimental study, and their thesis that when parents disagreed in party identification, mothers were more important than fathers in the transmission of party identification was later confirmed by Jennings and Langton (1969), in a study which was based upon a nationwide probability sample.

Our findings with respect to Japan are more complex. Table 4 indicates that in the first wave of the survey mothers emerge as the more effective influence on their children where the transmission of party identification is concerned, but that in the second wave this pattern is reversed and fathers have become the more important. A similar reversal of roles is found in the data from our mass survey as a whole.

Such a shift between the first and second waves of the survey was not unexpected. We are inclined to explain it along the following lines. The shift took place during a period of intense national campaigning. It is clear that in Japan men are both more interested in politics than women and that they more frequently participate in political activities. Under the circumstances it seems probable that the father is the principal agent of communication to the family of campaign and election messages from the outside world; in performing this function he increases the political solidarity of the household along the lines of his own partisan preferences.[18] Such a role would be analogous to that of the opinion-leader in the two-step theory of communications (Lazarsfeld et al., 1944: Chapter 16). In the Japanese case it also derives added plausibility from the importance

TABLE 4
CHILD'S AND FATHER'S OR MOTHER'S
PARTY IDENTIFICATIONS

	Pair Sample		Cross-Section Sample[a]	
Child's Party Identification in Agreement with:	First Wave	Second Wave	First Wave	Second Wave
Father's party identification	.22[b] (n = 23)	.49 (n = 27)	.36 (n = 625)	.38 (n = 694)
Mother's party identification	.54 (n = 43)	.29 (n = 36)	.42 (n = 357)	.32 (n = 423)

a. In the cross-section sample the father's and mother's party identifications are only indirectly measured (or based upon the child's report).
b. Entries are tau-b coefficients.

of what are called the *jiban* and *kankei* dimensions of their electoral system. A jiban is a bailiwick, a definable inhabited area linked by historic and complex interpersonal ties, that at election times tends to cast its vote as a unit ... the tendency varies a good deal with different levels of election (Beardsley et al., 1959: 424-445). Kankei in this sense are personal relations and refer to the intricate web of associations of family, interest, responsibility, and obligation that overlay any Japanese community (Flanagan, 1968). Both of these networks are routinely activated on the occasion of elections and their impact on a given family is apt to be channeled through the father. Their effect is to subject him to pressure to mobilize his family and other dependents in support of particular candidates or causes. The effect of these phenomena, we suspect, is a tendency to move other members of the family closer to the father in terms of political identification and thus to tilt the balance of relative importance in the father's favor at the later stages of or just after a lively and hard-fought election campaign.

It is not at all clear, however, that this short-span movement cancels the superiority of the mother in a longer-term sense. Certainly a straightforward interpretation of Table 4 would suggest that the mother is at least as important as the father as an agent for the generational transmission of party identification. Our interpretation inclines us to hypothesize that as the unusual psychological and sociological forces surrounding the campaign period recede into history, we may well find that the mother is normally the most effective agent of transmission.

If this is so, we are not certain as to why it should be the case. Japanese men are obviously more interested and more involved in politics than their wives. We suspect, however, that it may be a function of relative magnitude of exposure where the child is concerned. A child is normally more exposed to his mother's company and attentions than to his father's. Vogel (1967) makes an interesting case as to the quite pronounced degree to which this is so in middle-class Japanese families. Under these circumstances it seems highly probable that the mother in general is apt to have a greater effect on the socialization of the child. Where political socialization and in particular the transmission of party identification are concerned, it is not unlikely that such transmission is largely unintentional and unstructured, and that the mother is more apt to be the agent involved.

Jennings and Langton (1969: 342-344, 349-350) propose a similar hypothesis organized around the concept of closeness to parent. They argue that the closer a child feels to a particular parent, the more likely he is to be influenced by that parent; since a child is generally closer to his mother than to his father, the mother is apt to be more important than the father in the generational transmission of party identification. This concept of closeness approximates our concept of magnitude of exposure; although overlapping it in a number of respects, the former is really an attitudinal and the latter a more physical variable. A notable difference, however, is that while Jennings and Langton apply their concept to only those cases in which parental-party identifications are heterogeneous, we apply ours to all cases (Jennings and Langton, 1969; Jennings and Niemi, 1968: 181).

Unfortunately, in our survey we did not measure the extent to which a child feels close to his mother or to his father. The closest approximation thereto was our examination of the extent to which a child feels dependent upon or independent of his family in the making of critical life decisions.[19] The two dimensions are clearly different but overlapping in the sense that they both revolve about the child's attitudes toward parents or a parent, and in this case we are dealing with the child's normal attitudes toward his parents and not his emotionally charged attitudes toward parental authority. It may also be that to some extent the types of attitudes tapped by these two questions are interrelated. Under these circumstances, although the linkage is highly suppositious, it may be of some interest to hypothesize that the two variables represent two different ways of operationalizing the concept of magnitude of exposure in order to see what follows. If one then assumes that magnitude of exposure rather than sex of the parent is the critical factor in the generational transmission of party identification, we would expect the superiority of mother to father to vanish once we control for magnitude of exposure. In other words, if we control for the family-individual relation in our study (or for closeness to a particular parent in the Jennings-Langton study which was not done here), the extent of the agreement between the child's and the mother's party identifications should not be significantly greater than that between the child's and the father's party identifications. Our data indicate this to be the case. Because of sample size and the number and type of assumptions involved in the above reasoning, Table 5 obviously should be treated with caution, but the coefficients obtained are dramatically similar to the anticipated result were our assumptions to be valid.

Our data also provide an opportunity for cross-cultural comparison with respect to the degree to which a child's ability to recall his father's party identification affects the probability that the child himself will

TABLE 5
CHILD'S AND FATHER'S OR MOTHER'S PARTY IDENTIFICATIONS BY THE FAMILY-INDIVIDUAL RELATIONSHIP

Agreement of Party Identification between:	First Wave	Second Wave
Family-oriented child and:		
Father	1.00[a] (n = 5)	1.00 (n = 6)
Mother	1.00 (n = 6)	.84 (n = 8)
Individual-oriented child and:		
Father	-.31 (n = 16)	.18 (n = 18)
Mother	.40 (n = 33)	.13 (n = 27)

a. Entries are tau-b coefficients.

develop some sort of party identification of his own. Comparable data are provided for France and the United States by Philip E. Converse and George Dupeux (Campbell et al., 1966: 281-283). The resulting percentages, while not, of course, identical, are generally similar for the three countries and suggest a quite high degree of relationship between ability or inability to recall the father's party identification on the one hand, and the disposition of the child to acquire some form of party identification of his own. One suspects that such recall implies the presence and action of other generationally transmitted cues that are involved in the genesis and subsequent development of party identification by children. No claim is made in the case of such recall either that in fact the father did have a party identification or that the particular identification recalled is accurate. In this context of psychological dynamics, the perceived fact is normally more significant than the fact itself.

A final aspect of parental influence remaining to be examined is the effect of the homogeneity or heterogeneity of the parents' party identifications on the generational transmission of party identification.[20] As we have seen, both father and mother are important in the process, although in somewhat different degrees and ways. We would anticipate that in Japan as in the United States homogeneity of parental party identification would facilitate and heterogeneity impede generational transmission (Campbell et al., 1960: 146-148; Jennings and Langton, 1969: 333-341). Table 7 supports such a view.

We feel that the striking degree to which the coefficients in Table 7 support such a hypothesis is due in part to the fact that we relied upon

TABLE 6
RECALLING FATHER'S PARTY IDENTIFICATION AND RESPONDENT'S PARTY IDENTIFICATION
(in percentages)

	Know Father's Party			Do Not Know Father's Party		
	France[a]	USA[a]	Japan[b]	France	USA	Japan
Proportion having some partisan self-location (party or vague tendence)	79.4	81.6	85.0 87.9	47.7	50.7	61.1 64.9
Proportion that these are of total electorate	24.0	75.0	37.0 42.9	63.0	8.0	40.2 37.3

a. From Campbell et al. (1966: 282).
b. The first column of statistics are from the first wave, and the second column from the second wave of our cross-section survey.

indirect data in measuring the extent of parental homogeneity in this respect.[21] There is little question that children tend to overreport the degree of parental homogeneity and that this tendency inflates the statistical relationship involved. But in the Japanese case such a tendency does not seem great enough to affect the basic validity of our findings. Japanese children were found to overreport the extent of agreement between their own party identifications and those of their parents only in rather small degree, smaller than we anticipated, in fact.[22] It seems reasonable, therefore, to assume that the child's tendency to overreport homogeneity between the parents' party identifications is comparably

TABLE 7
GENERATIONAL TRANSMISSION OF PARTY IDENTIFICATION BY PARENTAL HOMOGENEITY[a]

Parental Homogeneity in Party Identification	Agreement between Child's and Parent's Party Identifications	
	First Wave	Second Wave
High	.67[b] (n = 27)	.49 (n = 34)
Low	-.32 (n = 9)	-.47 (n = 7)

a. Parental homogeneity is measured partly on a basis of indirect data.
b. Entries are tau-b coefficients.

small. In any event, given the spread between the coefficients in Table 7, it would be difficult to avoid the conclusion that parental homogeneity is a strong factor in the generational transmission of party identification.

What of the relationship between parental partisan homogeneity and the family-individual relationship? We reported earlier a strong association between the way in which the child perceives his relation to the family and the generational transmission of party identification. Now we find a similar relation between parental partisan homogeneity and such transmission. These are the two variables that, on the basis of our analysis, seem to be most significantly involved in the process of intergenerational transmission. How do they relate to one another? Is parental partisan homogeneity independent of the family-individual relationship? If so, does each of these variables affect generational transmission independently and cumulatively, or are they correlated? If so, does one of them maintain only a spurious relationship with the other in the generational transmission of party identification?

We find largely affirmative answers for the first of these sets of questions. The two variables are largely independent of each other. When we correlate parental partisan homogeneity and family-individual relationship, we obtain tau-b scores of −.04 and −.06 for our pair sample and .01 and .03 for our mass sample as a whole. Each of these variables also contributes to the process of generational transmission more or less independently and cumulatively. Except for the coefficient in the upper right-hand corner in the first-wave matrix, Table 8 is consistent with such a

TABLE 8
GENERATIONAL TRANSMISSION OF PARTY IDENTIFICATION BY PARENTAL PARTISAN HOMOGENEITY AND FAMILY-INDIVIDUAL RELATIONSHIP

Parental Homogeneity in Party Identification	First Wave Individual Oriented	First Wave Family Oriented	Second Wave Individual Oriented	Second Wave Family Oriented
High	.85[a] (n = 7)	.38 (n = 14)	.21 (n = 8)	.59 (n = 21)
Low	-1.00 (n = 2)	.41 (n = 3)	-.88 (n = 5)	.00 (n = 4)

a. Entries are tau-b coefficients.

supposition.[23] This is a view that, despite some differences in design and objective, would seem to be supported for the United States by the Jennings-Langton study.

CONCLUSION

Let us now reconsider one of the principal themes of the present paper, namely the surprising degree of similarity that seems to exist between Japan and the United States with respect to the aspects of the process of political socialization that we have investigated. Methodologically speaking, one reason for our emergence with such a finding is, of course, our obvious and extensive debt to American students of political socialization. We have borrowed liberally from and adapted to Japanese circumstances a variety of hypotheses and theories that have been developed in the course of what are obviously far more advanced and impressive studies than those available for any other single modern society. In tentative terms, at least, we are gratified by the results and encouraged to believe that the tactic should be more broadly and systematically applied to explorations of the process of political socialization in other advanced societies.

We would not wish, however, to be construed as predicting that the degree of cross-cultural similarity that we think we have detected in this quite limited investigation is also apt to obtain in most other areas of the Japanese political socialization process. We are too well aware that degrees of family influence on political socialization are more readily predictable and measurable than are the influences of most other socializing agencies and of the advantages that accrue from our having focused upon one of the most researchable and promising aspects of the socializing process, the generational transmission of party identification. We suspect that many other areas will not display a comparable degree of similarity, but the point is that we do not now know to what degree this is true. This being so, we are simply suggesting the value of an informed, systematic, and culturally sensitive adaptation of the relatively well-developed methodology and propositions of American scholarship in this field to the study of political socialization in other modern societies. One needs in comparative studies some sort of benchmark or point of departure. In practical terms there is much to be said for using the best-developed one available.

Before concluding, it might be well at this point to reiterate a few scattered earlier remarks about the basic character of our study. So far as political socialization is concerned, it is intended as a pilot study. This is true both in terms of its sampling design and of limitations on the data gathered. It is not comparable in either sense to a standard nationwide survey in Japan or the United States. Its goals are to explore neglected frontiers, to demonstrate feasibility, and to establish guidelines for and encourage the conduct of more definitive studies in the future, not to arrive itself at definitive conclusions. Of course we have also been interested in raising theoretical issues of broader scope about the role of the family and its members as agents of political socialization and in attempting to devise ways to operationalize such issues. We are aware that this interest has on occasion led us to quite liberal interpretations of some of the data. Still the constraints involved go far beyond those of the normal speculative study and the technical requirements of data analysis have been carefully followed. In this respect it has, of course, been possible to present only a very small proportion of the thousands of tabulations involved. The result, we hope, is a study that is more than speculative both in character and value.

With these qualifications in mind, we would like to comment on three aspects of the overall findings of this study:

(1) the extent of family influence in political socialization in Japan;
(2) the role of the family in the larger and overall process of political socialization and political change in Japan;
(3) problems associated with the study of political socialization in comparative and cross-cultural terms.

The study establishes a probability that in a particular area, the generational transmission of party identification, the Japanese family does play an important and demonstrable role. This is contrary to the view that, largely on the basis of speculative commentary, has come to be rather widely held among both Japanese and foreign scholars. It is notable also that the degree of influence found for Japan is similar to, although lower than, that held to prevail in the United States.

This does not mean that the influence of the family is either dominant or necessarily significant where other areas of the political-socialization process are concerned. In fact our data indicate that when the focus of inquiry shifts from party identification to issue orientations, family influence—at least for our fifteen- through nineteen-year bracket—seems to play only a marginal and negligible role (it might prove higher for younger age groups). This, too, is similar to the American case.

It is also of interest under this first rubric to note that when we look more intensively at the details of parental influence on children's party identifications, the role of the mother seems at least as prominent as that of the father, and possibly more so. This, too, resembles the American experience but with the addition of a more pronounced, if possibly temporary, role for the father in the later stages of electoral campaigns.

Turning to the role of the family in the larger and overall process of political socialization and political change in Japan, it is our interpretation that the extent of family influence is more limited. It was partly in this connection that we suggested the desirability of distinguishing between the impact of macroforces and microforces on individual attitudes and behavior. In this context, the family, of course, represents a microforce. The case of Japan is particularly interesting in this respect because the volume and intensity of major social, economic, and political changes have been so great during the last century as a whole and since World War II in particular.

Unfortunately, the absence of systematic survey data on public attitudes with respect to such changes and the very limited temporal dimensions of our own survey (the two waves were separated by only a few weeks) make it impossible to analyze the causality of such changes with any precision. Still it is obvious that, for example, on the war-peace dimension, the private-public welfare dimension, or the personal sacrifice and savings-personal-enjoyment dimension Japanese attitudes have changed markedly since the war. It is difficult in a positive sense to assign any significant share of the responsibility for such shifts to microforces such as the family. It is more the macroforces that seem to be involved, probably operating over time and largely through agents of socialization other than the family at the microlevel. Still there is also another facet to this picture of large-scale social change in postwar Japan, a facet featuring a greater element of continuity. One aspect of this is encountered in the realm of party identification. While it is true that there have been significant shifts in popular partisan orientations in connection with the rise of new parties since the war, it is also true that there have been notable continuities. The bulk of the Japanese electorate was conservative in their partisan identification before the war and they continue so today, although the spectrum of available choice has been very substantially expanded.

One is led to juxtapose these findings that in recent Japanese political history issue-oriented attitudes have tended to be relatively unstable and partisan-oriented attitudes relatively stable with the conclusion emerging from our data that the extent of generational transmission is small where issue-oriented attitudes are concerned, but relatively large where party identification is concerned. This suggests that the extent to which generational transmission takes place in political socialization may be related to the degree of stability manifested by the attitude or value in question over the historical dimension. If so, this is, of course, another way of saying that a microforce such as the family has with respect to this relatively stable phenomenon of party identification played a significant role in the longer-term process of political socialization and political change in Japan. The point obviously requires much further investigation, however.

Finally, a somewhat puzzled and indeterminate word about the problems of studying political socialization or other political phenomena in comparative and cross-cultural terms when the mode of study employed is the survey method. This was our approach and we like to think that the comparative content that was so obviously involved in our sampling design, questionnaire drafting, and theoretical suppositions has enriched the results and made them less remote approximations to the level of culture-free generalization about important political phenomena. But it is precisely the problems suggested by the intimidating compound adjective "culture-free" that continue to trouble us. Permit us to cite just two examples that, while certainly not novel, are characteristic of this sort of endeavor, especially where the terms of comparison involve cultures as historically disparate as those of Japan and the United States. Both are aspects of the problem of equivalence, one at the conceptual, the other more at the technical semantic or linguistic level.

Take the concept of party identification as the first example. There are obvious differences between the Japanese and American party systems. The United States has only two major national parties and these have been stable for many years. Japan now has five and has historically experienced a good deal of instability on her party scene. Party allegiance in Japan is also less stable and perhaps less salient than in the United States, although Japanese party orientations are somewhat more strongly correlated with actual partisan vote choices than in the American case. These are differences between the two systems. We can also find a good deal of common ground. Which is more significant where the concept of party identification is concerned? Is there a high enough degree of similarity to the concept across the two cultures to legitimate comparisons of the type we have been attempting, or are the differences more controlling? If the latter is valid, are there ways of adjusting for such differences? We really do not yet know, and in this sense something of an act of faith or at least an implicit request for a suspension of judgment is required in many such experiments. The problems may be less troublesome where more closely related cultures are involved.

Then there are a range of problems relating to the translation of questionnaires from English to Japanese and of the results back into English again. What degrees of freedom should be involved? Does one strive for literal accuracy in translation or for cultural equivalence, and if the latter, how can he tell when he really has it? It is quite remarkable how variant the judgments of so-called experts and bilinguals can be in these respects, especially when dealing with a language as remote from English and as intrinsically vague by western standards as ordinary spoken Japanese.

Unhappily, we have no simple answers for these questions. Our instinct and our endeavor have been to seek cultural equivalence. We are not, however, really certain that in all cases we obtained it and, when dealing with a technology such as survey research, one likes to be as certain as possible of the rigor and reliability of all his instruments. Cross-cultural research of this sort simply seems inherently to involve—under present circumstances at least—a somewhat greater degree of uncertainty on scores of this sort than does monocultural research. One imagines that such degrees of uncertainty may multiply as do the numbers of cultural elements involved. Such issues, of course, affect ultimately almost all aspects of a cross-cultural research project. The answers one gives to them condition the design and wording of the questionnaire, the quality of the responses elicited, and the data-anlysis process itself. Consequently, they merit very serious consideration.[24]

We seek to highlight these issues because of our impression that insufficient attention has been paid them so far in the design and conduct of cross-cultural survey research, and also because they caused us a good deal of concern in designing and administering our own survey. We would not like to leave the impression, however, that we consider them so serious that they need invalidate attempts to apply the survey method on a cross-cultural basis. Such attempts seem to us both essential and promising at this level for pretty much the same reasons advanced with respect to the application of survey methodology on the domestic scene. Where applicable, it lends itself to greater rigor, greater control, greater precision, and greater certainty than do more qualitative approaches. It is, furthermore, essential to the advancement of our capacities to make really generalized statements about political attitudes and behavior. It is wise to be aware, however, of the added pitfalls involved, and to give these the most serious attention.

NOTES

1. Recent studies of this subject in Japan (for example, Nishihira, 1964b) indicate that the JSP is losing support among the youngest cohorts of new voters. Nishihira's article was originally written in Japanese (1964a) and then translated into English (1964b). Japanese personal names cited in this paper are given in the Japanese manner; i.e., with surname first.

2. An antecedent to these factors may be the family's role as the main source of satisfaction for an infant's basic needs (Davies, 1965: 10-13).

3. Another way to examine this problem is to look at correlation coefficients

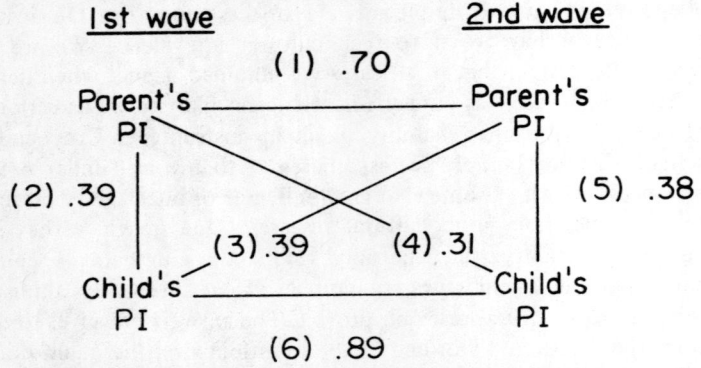

```
       1st wave                              2nd wave
                        (1) .70
         Parent's _____ Parent's
           PI  \                          / PI
                \                        /
   (2) .39       \                      /          (5) .38
                  \ (3) .39    (4) .31 /
                   X
         Child's  /                    \  Child's
           PI   _____   PI
                        (6) .89
```

among all combinations of the attitudes involved: In the above diagram we find two characteristics which support our supposition: (a) the coefficients for (2), (3), (4) and (5) are almost constant; and (b) the coefficient for (6) is very high. The relatively low coefficient for (1) is explained later in connection with Table 4.

4. Because of the difficulty in reliably pinning down the time point in the past in which the child was specifying his first party identification and the problems of parental recall associated therewith, we used the current status of parental-party identifications rather than some earlier status in running these correlations. Generally our data indicate little change over time in the past and present status of parents' party identifications.

5. We have encountered a similar recall problem in our attempt to measure generational agreement of party identification in our mass-survey data as a whole. Although the numerical values of these correlation coefficients (.38 for the first wave and .32 for the second wave) closely resemble those of the comparable coefficients for our parent-child pairs, the substantive relationship in the former is probably weaker than in the latter. Also the fact that the Japanese party system has been relatively unstable makes it very difficult to recover substantive relationships on the basis of perceived data alone.

6. It seems improbable that a perceived "fact" of this sort will in a statistical sense be totally different from the fact itself. In our Japanese data there is a high degree of agreement between the parent's report of his own party identification and the child's report of his parent's party identification:

	First Wave	Second Wave
Father	.64[a]	.81
Mother	.86[a]	.88

a. Entries are tau-b coefficients

7. Our figures do not exactly correspond to the figures cited by Nishihira Shigeki (1964b: 139), but it should be noted that the phrasing of our party-identification question is substantially different from that of Nishihira's. Also we see in both tables 1 and 2 that when parents are DSP identifiers, all of their children are LDP identifiers. This is obviously due to the small number of cases we find for this particular category.

8. Although it is difficult to compare issue attitudes crossculturally in any meaningful manner, it appears that Japanese more frequently say, "Don't know" to a standard-issue question than Americans. It is not unusual to find a 20% or 30% DK ratio in Japan, whereas in America a comparable ratio tends to remain in the 10-to-20% level and only occasionally surpasses the 20% mark.

9. Examples would be attitudes toward the Self-Defense Forces which scored .40 for the first wave and .20 for the second; or attitudes toward protesting official decisions on legitimate claims (.41), the power of big business (.47), or the power of labor unions (.49), all of which were measured only once.

10. Examples would be coefficients relating to the party which the respondent first liked (.55 and .45), party-vote intention (.42), and the ranking of the Democratic Socialist Party on a like-dislike scale (.40). There are currently five major national parties in Japan. There have been upwards of twenty in the 1945-1969 period alone.

11. A complicating factor in Japan is the existence of a multiparty system based on a system of multimember electoral districts. This may be conducive to an added degree of instability in party attitudes (see Ward, 1967: 52-75).

12. More specifically, we obtained the following tau-b coefficients:

	First Wave		Second Wave	
	High	Low	High	Low
Child's:				
Interest in election	.49	.10	.63	-.05
Concern with outcome	.54	.25	.50	.09
Political interest	.55	.20	.42	.03

13. The question used to measure this relationship is as follows: In dealing with such problems as education, occupation, and marriage, how do you make a decision? Which of the following statements comes closest to your opinion? (a) Decide on the basis of my own interests; (b) decide more or less on the basis of my own interests; (c) decide more or less on the basis of my family's interest; (d) decide on the basis of my family's interests; and (e) no opinion/DK.

14. The question used to measure this dimension is as follows: Would you say you are more or less a new type of person or an old type of person?

15. The question used to measure this dimension is as follows: Would you say you are the type of person who tends to save money or the type of person who tends to spend it so as to have a good time?

16. The questions used to measure these variables are as follows: Do you feel that today's youth need more discipline or not? Do you feel that today's youth should pay more respect to their parents' opinion or not?

17. We obtain the following tau-b correlation matrix:

	Family individual	New- or old-man	Youth discipline	Respect for parents' view
Family-individual	—			
New- or old-man	.184	—		
Youth discipline	-.093	-.104	—	
Respect for parents' view	-.109	-.106	.472	—

18. Our index of homogeneity increases in the following manner:

	High 1	2	3	Low 4	Total
First wave	57.3%	20.5	18.3	3.9%	100%
Second wave	70.5%	14.8	10.4	4.3%	100%

19. See note 13 above for the text of the question.

20. Parental homogeneity in party identification is measured in the following manner:

High *1.* Both parents are identified with the same major party. By a major party we mean either LDP, CGP, DSP, JSP, or JCP.

2. Both parents are independents or "others."

3. One of the parents is identified with one of the major parties, and the other is either an independent or "other."

Low *4.* Both parents are identified with different major parties.

----

0 One of the parents responded with either DK or NA.

21. Since our sample is based upon one-child-and-one-parent pairs rather than one-child-and-father-mother triples, we have no choice but to rely upon perceived data for information pertaining to the remaining parent.

22. See note 6.

23. Another way to interpret Table 8 is to argue that a clear-cut pattern we find in the second wave is due to the kind of problem we discussed with regard to Table 4 and that an ambiguous pattern we see in the first wave more accurately represents the relationship that we are trying to identify. Yet on the other hand, there is no question that at least the triangle at the lower left-hand corner of the first-wave coefficients supports our supposition; it is difficult to attribute the results in the second wave to campaigning entirely. This is the type of problem which we obviously need to explore further.

24. Some preliminary work has been carried out (Ervin et al., 1952-1953: 595-604; Almond et al., 1963: 43-76), but a great deal still needs to be done.

REFERENCES

ALMOND, G. A. and S. VERBA (1963) The Civic Culture: Political Attitudes and Democracy in Five Nations. Princeton: Princeton Univ. Press.
BEARDSLEY, R. K., J. W. HALL and R. E. WARD (1959) Village Japan. Chicago: Univ. of Chicago Press.
CAMPBELL, A., P. E. CONVERSE, W. E. MILLER and D. E. STOKES (1960) The American Voter. New York: John Wiley.
——— (1966) Elections and the Political Order. New York: John Wiley.
CONVERSE, P. E. (1964) "The nature of belief systems in mass publics," pp. 206-261 in David Apter (ed.) Ideology and Discontent. New York: Free Press.
——— (1966) "The problem of party distances in models of voting change," pp. 175-207 in M. Kent Jennings and L. Harmon Zeigler (eds.) The Electoral Process. Englewood Cliffs, N.J.: Prentice-Hall.
DAVIES, J. C. (1965) "The family's role in political socialization." Annals of Amer. Academy of Pol. and Social Sci. 361 (September): 10-19.
DAWSON, R. E. and K. PREWITT (1969) Political Socialization. Boston: Little, Brown.
DORE, R. P. (1958) City Life in Japan: A Study of a Tokyo Ward. London: Routledge & Kegan Paul.
ELKIN, F. (1960) The Child and Society. New York: Random House.
ERVIN, S. and R. T. BOWER (1952-1953) "Translation problems in international surveys." Public Opinion Q. 16 (Winter): 595-604.
FLANAGAN, S. C. (1968) "Voting behavior in Japan: the persistence of traditional patterns." Comparative Pol. Studies 1 (October): 391-412.
GREENSTEIN, F. I. (1965) Children and Politics. New Haven: Yale Univ. Press.
HESS, R. D. and J. V. TORNEY (1965) The Development of Basic Attitudes and Values Toward Government and Citizenship During the Elementary School Years, Part I. U.S. Office of Education.
——— (1967) The Development of Political Attitudes in Children. Chicago: Aldine.
HYMAN, H. (1959) Political Socialization. New York: Free Press.
JENNINGS, M. K. and K. P. LANGTON (1969) "Mothers versus fathers: the formation of political orientations among young Americans." J. of Politics 31 (May): 329-358.
——— and R. G. NIEMI (1968) "The transmission of political values from parent to child." Amer. Pol. Sci. Rev. 62 (March): 169-184.
KURODA, Y. (1965) "Agencies of political socialization and political change: political orientation of Japanese law students." Human Organization 24 (Winter): 328-331.
LAZARSFELD, P. F., B. BERELSON and H. GAUDET (1944) The People's Choice. New York: Duell, Sloan & Pearce.
LIFTON, R. G. (1962) "Youth and history: individual change in postwar Japan." Daedalus 91 (Winter): 172-197.
MACCOBY, E. E., R. E. MATHEWS and A. S. MORTON (1954) "Youth and political change." Public Opinion Q. 18 (Spring): 23-39.

NIEMI, R. G. (1967) A Methodological Study of Political Socialization in Family. Ph.D. dissertation. University of Michigan.
NISHIHIRA S. (1963) Nihonjin no iken. Tokyo: Seishindō.
——— (1964a) "Seinensō no hoshuka towa nanika." Asahi Jānuru 6 (July 26): 12-19.
——— (1964b) "Are young people becoming more conservative?" J. of Social and Pol. Ideas in Japan 1 (December): 137-143.
SPIRO, M. (1955) "The acculturation of American ethnic groups." Amer. Anthropologist 57 (December): 1240-1252.
VOGEL, E. F. (1967) "Kinship structure, migration to the city, and modernization," pp. 91-111 in R. P. Dore (ed.) Aspects of Social Change in Modern Japan. Princeton: Princeton Univ. Press.
WARD, R. E. (1967) Japan's Political System. Englewood Cliffs, N.J.: Prentice-Hall.

POLITICAL ORGANIZATION AND THE POLITICIZATION OF THE POBLADOR

DANIEL GOLDRICH

DANIEL GOLDRICH, *Professor of Political Science at the University of Oregon, is the author of SONS OF THE ESTABLISHMENT; ELITE YOUTH IN PANAMA AND COSTA RICA and co-author of THE RULERS AND THE RULED. He recently returned from 18 months in Chile and Peru on research with the Ford Foundation.*

This is a study of the effect of organization on the politicization of the poblador in some Santiago and Lima settlements. A poblador is an urban squatter or resident in a government settlement. The themes addressed are: variations in community-politicization patterns by national political structural factors, and by the stage of the community in the quest for housing security; the effect of sanctions on politicization, and the role of partisanship and party organization in assuaging that effect; the role of particular parties in promoting politicization, especially the Chilean Marxist parties in land-invasion situations; the special effect of these parties in the maintenance of solidarity after the attainment of housing and urban facilities, and in the shift in focus of politicization to economic needs. A conglomerate case history is presented of the political organization of the homeless in Santiago by the Communist party. This illustrates the interaction of organization in a situation of acute need to politicize previously apolitical adults, intensely and for a considerable period, despite severe hardship and sanction. The general significance of political organizations in relation to acute needs as politicizing factors is then considered, with additional reference to the Cuban revolutionary situation.

If the definition of political socialization is taken to be "the process by which an individual learns politically relevant attitudinal dispositions and behavior patterns" (Langton, 1969: 5) then the link here between the study of political socialization and that of politicization is the focus on the effect of a set of political factors (such as party organization and the political structuring of the ways of meeting needs) on the political involvement of the poblador. Any significance this study may have derives from two considerations: (1) political socialization generally has been studied in relation to childhood and early youth, whereas the present

---

AUTHOR'S NOTE: *Support for this reported research came from the Ford Foundation and from the Social Science Research Council.*

report focuses on adult socialization; (2) most theoretical and research attention has been given to such relatively nonpolitical politicizing agents as the family and school, while the present study focuses on political organization and political situations as politicizing agents.

BACKGROUND[1]

This is a study of residents of four lower-class settlements on the urban periphery of Santiago, Chile, and Lima, Peru. All four have been recently established, are permanent, and have obtained or are in the process of obtaining legal title to the land. Three have their origins in squatter invasions. The fourth is a government housing project, partly composed of invaders and of applicants who successfully qualified through a "normal" administrative process. These areas are commonly stereotyped by more prestigious elements within the nation as slums, but they are in reality being improved and consolidated, and as such should be sharply distinguished from deteriorating areas or true slums.

The data are derived largely from interviews conducted with samples of lower-class male adult residents of the four communities during the period of May through July, 1965. Additional background information was collected prior to and after the surveys.

In the two Santiago areas, a very recent census was available from which households and respondents within them were randomly selected. In the two Lima barriadas, block and dwelling maps were used to assign areas to interviewers, who selected households and respondents by availability, although care was taken to disperse the selection throughout the area. The representativeness of our sample in the El Espíritu barriada is indicated by its close congruence in important respects such as education, with the sample characteristics of another, more systematically designed study done there in the same year (Instituto de Investigaciones Económicas, 1965).

THE FOUR RESEARCH COMMUNITIES

The two barriadas on Lima's outskirts originated in organized invasions of undeveloped state-owned land. Pampa Seca was thus founded without active opposition in 1957, while El Espíritu's origin in 1962 was violently confronted by the police. Though both have made considerable physical progress, Pampa Seca is the much more established of the two. Its population at the time of the study was about 30,000; that of El Espíritu, about 14,000.

In 1960, 3 de Mayo (May 3) was established by invasion with little public notice in the Santiago periphery. After years of negotiation the settlement won a presumption of legal permanence from the government, and expected future large-scale assistance in home construction and urban facilities for its approximately 1,200 residents.

Santo Domingo was created in 1961 as one of the new low-cost government housing projects in the periphery of the working-class districts. It has two main types of residents, those recruited through normal administrative processes (about 70%), and those who invaded public lands and were then transferred to the project (about 30%). Legal title will be given to the residents upon completion of relatively low monthly payments on a long-term mortgage. Santo Domingo had about 12,000 residents and the best physical facilities of the four communities.

The great majority of people in these communities have had years of metropolitan experience, though originally rural and provincial. Educationally and occupationally they represent a range of urban lower-class situations, but rank well above the bottom typically. Compared to their fathers, the men in these samples are considerably more educated and better off occupationally.

POLITICIZATION: CONCEPT AND MEASUREMENT

In this study, the concept of politicization refers to the individual's awareness and psychological involvement in politics, his image of himself as an active or passive agent in it, the accessibility to him of channels leading to political decision-making, and his participation directly in politics. The four components, then, are salience, sense of efficacy, access, and participation. The measure of this relationship to politics is the politicization scale.

A typology of politicization was constructed on these four bases with survey data. (The subscales are described in the Appendix.) Since active participation is here considered the behavior that has most impact on the political process, and a logical culmination of political involvement, the highest type, D, is defined thereby. It is assumed that active participants also have some medium attitudinal or access resource, and in fact that is the case. Pobladores of the D-type are referred to also as activists or demand makers. Type C includes those who are relatively highly politicized but have not actively participated; they may be moderately politicized on all four dimensions, or highly politicized on salience, efficacy, or access dimensions. Type B includes those who show medium politicization along two or three dimensions. Type A, the lowest, is characterized by either a total lack of development on any dimension, or medium development on a single one of them. For present purposes, relationships among the dimensions will be ignored. Suffice it to say here that activism is undergirded by varying patterns of salience, efficacy, and access. There is a strong monotonic relationship in each community between each of these dimensions and activism. Activism does not occur without at least medium development of some other dimension. Except for El Espíritu, 90 to 95% of the sets of activists show more than medium development along at least one of the dimensions.

THE POLITICIZATION OF THE POBLADORES

In three of the four cases, there is a higher incidence of activism than noninvolvement, demonstrating the distinctiveness of these settlements—despite their poverty and relatively poor physical conditions—from the archetypal slum with its attendant apathy. The high level of social organization, with which Mangin (1967) characterizes Latin American squatter settlements generally and which has also been cited for these four communities (Goldrich et al., 1967), has its reflection here in political terms. In the one case where there is a relative abundance of the A-type, the El Espíritu barriada, the phenomenon seems a probable consequence of a set of political factors to be analyzed, not of low socioeconomic resources.

Politicization varies along national lines, the Chilean pair of poblaciones having more residents in the higher categories than the Peruvian pair. Thus

TABLE 1
LEVELS OF POLITICIZATION, BY COMMUNITY

| | Politicization Type, In Percentages ||||||
	A (low)	B	C	D (high)	Total %	n
Lima						
Pampa Seca	20	28	28	24	100	(127)
El Espíritu	31	25	24	20	100	(119)
Santiago						
Santo Domingo—Total	15	19	40	27	101	(191)
Invaders	15	15	36	34	100	(59)
Noninvaders	14	20	42	24	100	(132)
3 de Mayo	11	21	28	40	100	(98)

there is an association between the structure and content of national politics (the major partisan competition between the Christian Democrats and the FRAP, and the prominence of economic- and social-policy issues such as popular housing) and the response of the poblador.

The least physically developed, least legally established, and socio-economically lowest of the settlements, 3 de Mayo, is by a substantial margin the most politicized. Four of every ten men are activists, and there are four times more of the D- than the A-type. Since the national political structure is the same for both Santiago settlements, and the partisan distribution is about the same in each, the critical factor seems to be the fact that the priority need of the pobladores, housing, is highly concrete in the Chilean context, with two of the major political forces having defined alternative solutions and fiercely competing for the support of this sector. Thus, need, the seizure of land, and responsive political organizations seem to have had far more effect as politicizers than physical and social deprivation as impediments.

That the factor of relative need alone is insufficient for high politicization is indicated by the low profile in El Espíritu, the Peruvian counterpart to 3 de Mayo in the sense of being the much-less-developed settlement of the pair.

Santo Domingo's politicization profile is higher than the Peruvians' but not nearly so high as 3 de Mayo's. Given the relative similarity in background between the two Santiago sets of pobladores, and the key role of the housing political process, a reasonable assumption is that Santo Domingo's politicization may once have been as high as 3 de Mayo's and has now diminished to its present level. Regarding the two types of residents (according to the process by which they acquired a place in the settlement), it may be expected that higher initial risk, internal organization, external support, and cost were involved for the invaders than in the case of those recruited through normal administrative processes. The hypothesis is that such an invasion process is an especially politicizing experience.

In fact, the proportion of activists among the Santo Domingo invaders is higher than among the other residents, approaching that of 3 de Mayo. Even after the provision of urban facilities and the acquisition of definitive housing, the invaders still show relatively high political involvement. But it is still notable, nevertheless, that the politicization level does not equal that of those not yet benefited. Why hasn't the demand level been sustained or escalated? All needs are not felt equally, and the housing problem was a case of a particularly deeply felt need. Housing is a highly tangible matter, the attainment of which is easy for the poblador to visualize; and the major political competitors in Chile had made this an issue, detailing alternative, plausible means of meeting the need. In other areas of severe need, such as sheer economic want, alternative courses of action were not so easily conceived nor so plausibly structured by the various sets of political leaders. This last factor will be examined subsequently regarding economic needs.

THE LAGGING POLITICIZATION OF EL ESPÍRITU

This barriada lags behind all the rest in politicization. There are no educational-, occupational-, income- or migrational-background differences between this and other settlements that might account for this profile. What does vary between El Espíritu and the other communities are the external and internal political circumstances surrounding their establishment. The response by the authorities to the original invasions varied. The 3 de Mayo seizure occurred quietly, and the government came later to negotiate a settlement between invaders and landowner. The invaders who later won a place in Santo Domingo were subjected to close police surveillance and constraint but not to violent suppression, though they were forcibly removed from the first site they had originally seized. Pampa Seca also was invaded without provoking a violent government reaction. El Espíritu, on the other hand, was the scene of a series of pitched battles between troops and squatters, involving some loss of life and property. In addition, the armed forces ringed the area for some time after the initial invasion so that the squatters were under constant fear that attacks would be launched to drive them off the land.

We have some survey evidence bearing on this matter for the two barriadas. The respondents were asked what problems they encountered in establishing themselves. Only 8% of the Pampa Seca sample referred to traumatic experiences with police or soldiers, but 42% of the El Espíritu sample mentioned the fighting, the encirclement, the necessity for posting night guard, and so on. In the context of this kind of background and survey data on the four settlements, we conclude that El Espíritu suffered a distinctively severe sanction.

One test of the impact of these special circumstances is the comparison of politicization profiles between original invaders and latercomers in the two barriadas, and between the invaders (the first actual residents) and duly administratively recruited residents of Santo Domingo.[2] Given (1) the typical preparation of groups planning invasion, including the important matter of taking into account the probable reaction of the relevant authorities; and (2) the heightened politicization of the immediate postinvasion period when essential services and legitimacy must be sought—entailing relatively intense dealing with officials—it is expected that the original invaders would be more politically involved than the latercomers.

The profiles are as expected in two of the three cases. Especially in Pampa Seca, but also in Santo Domingo, the original invaders are more politicized. In El Espíritu, however, there is essentially no such internal difference. Furthermore, its original invaders are much more heavily weighted toward the lowest end of the scale than the Pampa Seca counterparts.

If severe negative sanctions depoliticize, how do they do so and whom do they most affect? One of the distinctions noted above in original invasion circumstances was the degree of external support. In the two barriadas, there was none, at least in any overt organized fashion. But the invaders who finally achieved sites in Santo Domingo went through a protracted struggle for it, during which considerable support was organized, principally by the Communists and Socialists, but also by Christian Democrats. We expect that external support at a time of great stress contributes to the capacity to withstand that stress without subsequent depoliticization. We can test this in the case of support by

TABLE 2
POLITICIZATION OF ORIGINAL INVADERS VERSUS LATERCOMERS[a] IN THREE POBLACIONES

| | Politicization Type, in Percentages ||||||
	A	B	C	D	Total %	n
Pampa Seca						
Original Invaders	13	36	28	23	100	(61)
Latercomers	42	21	15	21	99	(33)
El Espíritu						
Original Invaders	30	26	24	20	100	(89)
Latercomers	26	26	26	22	100	(27)
Santo Domingo						
Original Invaders	15	15	36	34	100	(59)
Latercomers	14	20	42	24	100	(132)

a. In the case of the two barriadas, the total does not equal total sample size because two sets of respondents were eliminated from the particular analysis: those who failed to give sufficient information to permit assignment to one or another category, and those whose responses were too ambiguous to permit clearcut assignment.

parties by comparing the politicization of nonaffiliated versus partisan affiliates among the invaders.

The hypothesis is that sanctions particularly depoliticize those unaffiliated with outside political groups. Organization should help to withstand sanctions. If so, the nonaffiliated should show the least politicization in El Espíritu where the most severe sanctions occurred, the most in Pampa Seca where no sanctions occurred, and medium in Santo Domingo where moderate sanctions occurred. The evidence supports this, both in absolute comparisons among the three sets of nonaffiliates, and in a comparison of the strength of the relationship within each community between affiliation and politicization. El Espíritu's nonaffiliated are the least politicized of the three sets, and fall the farthest behind the affiliates; Pampa Seca's nonaffiliates are the most politicized, and the closest in politicization to the affiliates.

That sanctions can be withstood through organization is no surprise. What was unexpected is the almost equal support provided by party affiliation among the El Espíritu invaders compared to the Santo Domingo invaders, when in the latter community party politicians were so much in evidence, whereas in El Espíritu, there was little overt organized help. This suggests that the merest organizational tie-in to the establishment, to the powerful, is a strong psychological support for the poor in a time of political stress.

PARTIES, PARTISANSHIP AND POLITICIZATION

The general importance of parties in the politicization of the pobladores has already been indicated. This factor will now be examined more directly. A brief description of the party system provides background.

During the study period, both countries had popularly elected governments and multiparty systems. Chile had a wide spectrum ranging from Socialists on the farther left to Communists; the two allied in the FRAP coalition, Christian Democrats, Radicals; and on the farther right, the Nationals. Frei and the Christian Democrats did very well in the 1964 and 1965 elections. Since then, competition from the FRAP has kept pace, and there has been a resurgence on the right. Both the FRAP parties and the Christian Democracy (CD) have highly developed programs for political, social, and economic change. They vary between a seeking for more independence of the United States in foreign policy and economic

TABLE 3
POLITICIZATION OF PARTISAN AFFILIATES AND NONAFFILIATES AMONG ORIGINAL INVADERS IN THREE COMMUNITIES

	Politicization Type, in Percentages					
	A	B	C	D	Total %	n
Pampa Seca						
Nonaffiliated	18	43	27	12	100	(33)
Party Affiliates	7	29	29	36	101	(28)
El Espíritu						
Nonaffiliates	54	33	9	4	100	(46)
Party Affiliates	5	19	39	37	100	(43)
Santo Domingo						
Nonaffiliated	42	21	21	16	100	(19)
Party Affiliates	2	12	43	43	100	(40)

matters, and total rejection of United States dominance. The FRAP wants to move toward a nationalized economy, while the CD, though ideologically committed to communitarianism, is much more ambivalent about the role of private capital. However, the CD government has moved from joint state-United States company control of the copper mines to nationalization. Both the FRAP and the CD concern themselves with massive housing plans, agrarian reform, and educational expansion.

The major Peruvian parties cannot be arrayed so readily on a programmatic basis. Acción Popular of President Belaúnde (elected in 1963) had an image of progressiveness and of a technician-directed attack on underdevelopment. Its program was diffuse and its organization weak. APRA (American Popular Revolutionary Alliance) has long been led by Haya de la Torre, one of Latin America's major politicians. The APRA has been the best-organized party, once quite radical and the bête noire of the Peruvian establishment, now moderated to the point of conservatism in an effort to win the presidency and be allowed to govern by its traditional military opposition. The third party is the Unión Nacional Odriista (UNO), the traditionally, personalistically styled following of former dictator Manuel Odría. UNO and APRA coalesced after the 1963 election, and together controlled the legislature, preventing Belaúnde from carrying out much of his program. A fourth, small Peruvian party was Christian Democracy. Its support of Belaúnde was crucial in the 1963 election. The party had some substantial political leaders, but lacked impetus and organization; it split in two.

The inability of the Belaúnde government to forestall an economic crisis, its apparently compromised position regarding nationalization of the symbolically potent International Petroleum Company, and its internal division, making likely an APRA victory in the 1969 elections, prompted the military coup of October, 1968.

The greater programmatic focus on the poor of the Chilean Christian Democrats and Marxist parties is reflected in the receptivity of the pobladores. With the slightest exception, they affiliate only with these parties, and a much higher proportion affiliates than in the Peruvian communities. The Christian Democrats have recruited far more successfully than any of the other parties, a success demonstrated at the polls in the 1964 presidential and 1965 congressional elections. The design of this study has not generated data adequate to explain their appeal, but the fact that their program included a strong appeal to the poor and that the gains were projected without coercion, conflict, and disorder may account for their differential appeal compared to the FRAP, especially given the fact that the pobladores have just achieved, or are about to, property ownership for the first time in their lives.

The partisan politicization profiles indicate that any party affiliation tends to support political involvement. As noted previously regarding the El Espíritu case, even the Acción Popular and APRA in Peru seem to function in this regard though lacking a programmatic focus on the barriadas' problems; the FRAP parties with their more direct involvement in this area and their zealous activity in invasion cases seem to promote politicization most effectively. The apparent weakness of the Christian Democrats as a politicizing agent is somewhat offset by a consideration of their unsurpassed recruitment success. A part of that success may have been their capacity to mobilize for electoral purposes relatively apolitical people.

If indicators of local politicization are extracted from subscales of the overall politicization scale, rescored,[3] and combined into a local politicization scale, it provides a more refined reflection of the manner in which party organization tends to operate in these settlements.

The most outstanding aspect of the local profile is the high level of involvement of the FRAP invaders compared to all other groups. The significance of the association between FRAP organization and the invasion experience as a politicizing agent is indicated by the differentially high local involvement of FRAP invader groups compared to (1) FRAP noninvaders, and (2) Christian Democrat and nonaffiliated invaders, who either do not develop or do not sustain high local politicization. The interaction between party organization and the situation of homelessness leading to invasions is described in some case material (see Table 5).

TABLE 4
POLITICIZATION BY PARTY IN THE FOUR COMMUNITIES

	Politicization Type, in Percentages						
	A	B	C	D	Total %	n	% of tot. samp. affil. w/ea. party
Pampa Seca							
Nonaffiliated	30	33	24	13	100	(70)	55
Accion Popular	11	25	25	39	100	(28)	22
APRA	8	23	23	46	100	(13)	10
UNO	9	18	45	27	99	(11)	9
Other	—	—	—	—	—	(5)	4
El Espíritu							
Nonaffiliated	55	32	8	5	100	(63)	53
Accion Popular	0	17	37	46	100	(24)	20
APRA	0	9	36	55	100	(11)	9
UNO	11	22	44	22	99	(18)	15
Other	—	—	—	—	—	(3)	3
Santo Domingo							
Nonaffiliated	34	25	25	15	99	(67)	35
Christian Democracy	4	18	54	24	100	(83)	44
FRAP	3	9	40	49	101	(35)	18
Other	—	—	—	—	—	(6)	3
Santo Domingo—Invaders							
Nonaffiliated	42	21	21	16	100	(19)	32
Christian Democracy	4	18	52	26	100	(23)	39
FRAP	0	7	33	60	100	(15)	26
Other	—	—	—	—	—	(2)	3
Santo Domingo—Noninv.							
Nonaffiliated	31	27	27	15	100	(48)	36
Christian Democracy	3	18	55	23	99	(60)	46
FRAP	5	10	45	40	100	(20)	15
Other	—	—	—	—	—	(4)	3
3 de Mayo							
Nonaffiliated	28	28	22	22	100	(32)	33
Christian Democracy	2	24	41	33	100	(42)	43
FRAP	4	8	13	75	100	(24)	24

TRANSITION IN POLITICIZATION FROM HOUSING TO ECONOMIC NEEDS: THE ROLE OF THE PARTY

Dwelling and urbanization politics is characterized by the immediacy of the need, the tangibility of the goal, and the relative feasibility of the alternative solutions proposed by the major political competitors. Other objectively significant areas of need, such as economics and education, lack some or all of these characteristics. Consequently, politicization may

TABLE 5
LOCAL POLITICIZATION BY PARTY

	Local Politicization Score[a] in Percentages					
	0	1	2	3+	Total %	n
Pampa Seca						
Nonaffiliated	53	24	17	6	100	(70)
Accion Popular	50	25	25	0	100	(28)
APRA	23	62	0	15	100	(13)
UNO	27	46	18	9	100	(11)
El Espíritu						
Nonaffiliated	51	36	11	2	100	(63)
Accion Popular	12	54	12	21	99	(24)
APRA	9	64	18	9	100	(11)
UNO	28	67	0	6	101	(18)
Santo Domingo—Total						
Nonaffiliated	64	27	8	2	101	(67)
Christian Democracy	60	27	11	2	100	(83)
FRAP	31	31	23	14	99	(35)
Santo Domingo—Invaders						
Nonaffiliated	58	26	11	5	100	(19)
Christian Democracy	57	26	13	4	100	(23)
FRAP	20	20	27	34	101	(15)
Santo Domingo—Noninv.						
Nonaffiliated	67	27	6	0	100	(48)
Christian Democracy	62	26	10	2	100	(60)
FRAP	40	40	20	0	100	(20)
3 de Mayo						
Nonaffiliated	44	41	9	6	100	(32)
Christian Democracy	43	45	10	2	100	(42)
FRAP	25	17	21	37	100	(24)

a. Two items concerning participation in the local association and discussion of politics with friends and neighbors provide the basis of this measure. Leadership in the local association was given two points, membership one point; frequent political discussion was given two points, occasional discussion one point.

be less likely to develop in these areas, and may subside when the more acute dwelling and urbanization needs are met.

One way of assessing whether the poblador's politicization is likely to be sustained is to see what areas of potential demands, for example, are reflected by those who have already exhibited a high level of politicization. To the extent that they reveal little orientation toward other problem areas, it may be projected that their presently high degree of politicization will probably diminish. This would seem particularly the case in those poblaciones where dwelling and urbanization needs have been most fully met—particularly Santo Domingo, and then Pampa Seca.

Potential demands are measured here by a question asking "What could you do if you wanted to get the government to do something? What sorts of problems could you deal with this way? "[4]

By a considerable margin, Santo Domingo activists (37%) lead all others in indicating they could make demands concerning their economic and educational needs; they are followed by Pampa Seca (23%), 3 de Mayo (18%), and far behind, El Espíritu (4%). Thus in both the Santiago and Lima cases, there is evidence among the activists of a greater shift in focus from housing to broader economic (and educational) problem areas in the more established poblaciones. But since activists in both the more and the less established Santiago poblaciones evidence this shift more than their Lima counterparts, it seems that Chilean politics is also a factor.

A closer inquiry into the basis of the relatively pronounced development of economically oriented potential demands of Santo Domingo activists reveals that neither the factor of the high level of physical development of the settlement nor a general "Chilean politics" factor accounts for the phenomenon. There is an extremely powerful partisan factor, without which the level of economically based potential demands would fall to about that of the Pampa Seca activists. Some 59% of Santo Domingo activists affiliated with FRAP conceive of taking economic or educational problems before officials for help, compared to only 20% of the Christian Democrats.

Furthermore, the same indication occurs in 3 de Mayo. Though it is in far more precarious housing and urbanization circumstances than Santo Domingo, and therefore the potential demands of its activists are heavily weighted toward that area of problems, there is an extreme partisan difference regarding the substance of political discussion engaged in by these activists. Fully half of the FRAP affiliates report discussing economic issues, compared to but 7% of the Christian Democrats.[5]

No Peruvian partisan group shows an economic potential beyond that of the Chilean Christian Democrats. Though both parties ideologically stress economic issues as they affect the poor, it is only the FRAP that seems to socialize the poblador activist to think specifically about these matters in demand terms. And it is only the FRAP that has seemed to effect the transition in the politicization of the activist from the immediate, pressing housing need to a focus on more fundamental problems.

PROSPECTS FOR SOLIDARITY, AND THE ROLE OF PARTY

During the initial stage of poblacion establishment and conquest of basic urban services, a process that may last many years, there is a strong impetus to cohesive action. Toward the end of this stage, it becomes problematic whether the pobladores either can or will find reason to maintain their solidarity. To the extent that it lapses, they are much less likely to have an impact on the economic and political situations which they may want to affect. In the following, then, we focus on the general disposition of the pobladores to work collectively on the problems they face, and on the manner in which this factor is associated with politicization, education, and partisanship. The data came from responses to the question, "Do you believe that (1) families can resolve their problems by themselves; or (2) that they have to work with others and depend on one another to resolve them?" The first alternative is taken as an indicator of an individualistic orientation to problem-solving, and the second as indicating a disposition to work collectively.

There is really no variation of significance within pairs of poblaciones regarding disposition to work collectively; the major difference is a national one, the Peruvian barriadas displaying more of this disposition. Given the national differences in extent to which the governments have taken responsibility for meeting housing-urbanization needs of the poor, the greater emphasis on collective action in Peru is not so surprising. If anything is to be won, it must be primarily through the residents' own efforts.

There is a relationship in all communities between politicization and disposition to work collectively, though it varies in strength and there are minor deviations. Apparently, as the poblador becomes more aware of and involved in politics, he comes to perceive that some degree of interdependence promotes the resolution of his problems.

Given this relationship, however, the most highly politicized Santo Dominicans show much less collectivity disposition than any other set of D scorers. This is significant because Santo Domingo is the community among the four that has come closest to attaining the full complement of housing and urbanization facilities. Thus, the relatively low collectivity disposition of its highly politicized may augur a general decline in this orientation with increasing urbanization, at least on the part of the politically most demanding group, the activists. To the extent this is so, the poblador sector is likely to lose political impact in the degree to which its needs—narrowly defined in housing-urbanization terms—are fulfilled. The remaining fundamental economic problems, for example, would not be the object of the solidary action tending to occur in the case of the other needs.

TABLE 6
DISPOSITION TO WORK COLLECTIVELY, BY COMMUNITY, EDUCATION, AND PARTY

	Pampa Seca	El Espíritu	Sto. Dgo.	3 de Mayo
Percentage disposed to work collectively	60	65	42	48
Percentage disposed to work collectively by politicization level:				
A	42	69	29	9
B	63	57	42	29
C	69	61	46	59
D	61	75	45	62
Within D level, percentage partisans disposed to work collectively:[a]				
Christian Democrats	–	–	30	–
FRAP	–	–	53	–
Percentage disposed to work collectively by education:				
0-2 yrs. primary	68	67	49	37
Intermed. primary	52	70	49	52
Complete primary	58	61	42	48
Any secondary	68	64	26	54
Within D level, percentage disposed to work collectively by education:[b]				
Less than secondary	–	–	53	–
Any secondary	–	–	23	–
Within secondary-education level percentage disposed to work collectively by party:[c]				
Christian Democrat	–	–	13	–
FRAP	–	–	50	–

a. N of D-level Christian Democrats on which percent is based = 20, of FRAP, 17.
b. N of D-level secondary educated on which percent is based = 13, of less than secondary, 38.
c. N of secondary-educated Christian Democrats on which percent is based = 15, of FRAP = 8.

Once again, however, as in the case of the poblador's transition of political focus from the housing-urbanization syndrome to the economic, there is a party factor here. Among the highly politicized Santo Dominicans, the FRAP adherents show a markedly greater collectivity disposition than the Christian Democrats. As before, one notes the differential political socialization of the activist poblador, such that the parties of the FRAP tend to promote transition in focus to other problem areas, and maintenance of the collective orientation toward problem-solving.

Education may be a crucial factor with regard to disposition to work collectively. There is growing awareness in a country such as Chile that the effect of secondary education is to inculcate middle-class values in the young poblador, for which secondary education typically fails to provide the means of implementation, but which also psychologically removes the mobile, advantaged youth from any identification with his poblacion (Gurrieri, 1966).

There is no general relationship between education and collectivity orientation in the four communities. In three of the communities, the secondary educated either show more of this disposition or about the same degree of it as those less educated. However, in Santo Domingo the high school educated stand out as the least collectively oriented in their community, and compared to their relatively highly educated counterparts in the other communities, they are a great deal less disposed to work with each other. Furthermore when one looks at the effect of secondary education within the D-politization stratum in Santo Domingo, one sees that it strongly offsets the previously mentioned tendency of the more highly politicized toward a collectivity disposition. Even though the numbers are small, it seems extremely noteworthy that among the D's only 23% of the high school educated are disposed to work collectively, compared to 53% of the less educated.

The significance of this lies in its indication that the most educated (also both scarce and potentially most socially effective) pobladores may become increasingly individualistic in pursuit of their goals once the housing-urbanization needs are close to being met. Furthermore, though it is widely assumed that the increasing access of the poor to high school education is a progressive and totally desirable phenomenon in Latin America, this pattern suggests a consequence that is dysfunctional to the political solidarity required for breakthroughs in fundamental problem areas.

Here again there is evidence of a distinctive partisan factor, the consistency of which tends to override my caution because of the small numbers on which this analysis is made. Fully half of the high school educated affiliated with the FRAP are disposed to work collectively, compared to only 13% of the Christian Democrats at the same educational level. In their function as agents of political socialization, the parties of the FRAP seem able to offset the individualizing impact of high school education, in strong distinction to Christian Democracy. Though both parties at the leadership level promote ideologies valuing organization and collective action of the poor, only the FRAP seems to effect the internalization of this principle in its poblador adherents.

The survey data provide evidence that any organizational affiliation helps support the poor through a taxing process of making a political demand. Affiliation even with parties as unrelated to the general problems of the poor as the Peruvian ones is associated with a relatively high degree of politicization, though the more direct, on-the-scene character of the FRAP parties is reflected in the even higher politicization of the invader groups they supported. Beyond this, the Chilean data provide evidence that the activist poor who support the FRAP tend to maintain a sense of solidarity and make the transition, in their thinking, about politics from the acute housing need focus to the equally acute but less vulnerable set of economic needs.

But this solidarity and disposition to consider economic demand-making has not been reflected in action. Why not? The housing needs were acute, a line of easily imaginable action existed through which to meet the needs, involving an organization through which to mobilize the people themselves and external support. But for economic needs, the situation is different. Few clearcut lines of action have been formulated by the FRAP or any other party leadership indicating what the poor might do to change their economic condition other than to give them electoral support. This point will be raised again in the concluding section.

This analysis of the marked effectiveness of the FRAP in politicizing the pobladores derives from survey data collected at one point in time. A less systematic but more dynamic description of the manner in which the FRAP relates to the housing needs of the poor and mobilizes their political participation adds a different kind of evidence about its functioning.

THE POLITICIZATION OF "LOS SIN CASA"

The situation of many "los sin casa" (homeless) groups in greater Santiago provides evidence calling for a reconsideration of political socialization theory.[6] The los sin casa are extremely poor, young families who in increasing thousands as organized collectivities pressure the government for a housing solution. They engage in a political process of demand-making and complex pressure-building over an intense period of sometimes two years, which may culminate in an illegal act of land invasion frequently met with force—in any event, involving severe hardship. Throughout, their political behavior demonstrates a capacity for organization, discipline, and purposeful sacrifice (Giusti, 1968). Key factors seem to be an acute need, and a perceived way of meeting this need through political organization. The political and theoretical significance lie therein too, since the phenomenon shows that thousands of people, ordinarily considered to be lacking the experiences and resources to sustain concerted political action, learn to do so where their needs can be met. The focus then should shift to the general question, under what conditions is such behavior elicited?

The los sin casa are the following: families, perhaps having recently come from the provinces, living with relatives in a room; those dispossessed from center-city rooms scheduled for demolition for urban improvements; squatters on marginal lands; and renters of costly, cramped, inadequate quarters. The demand on government has also been reinforced by the fact that since so much of the lower class live in government projects, their married children and other relatives temporarily living with them come to expect an expansion of public efforts in their own behalf.

Typically the formation of a demand for housing is the first protracted political experience for the homeless. Most have only a primary education and have therefore been outside the politicizing environment of the secondary school. Nor does any union affiliation seem to involve the young men politically by this stage in their lives. Many hold marginal jobs, and the level of unemployment among them is high.

The seizure of land for homesites is a common third-world and Latin American occurrence (Abrams, 1966). In the greater Santiago area, organized land invasions on a large scale have been increasing in number ironically as successive governments have devoted increasing resources to popular housing problems. The Alessandri administration (1958-1964) engaged in large-scale construction of housing settlements for the poor, but the cost of this approach of providing definitive housing and urbanization was too great for either a conservative government such as Alessandri's, or even a reformist government such as Frei's; the latter largely discontinued the program. Frei shifted to Operación Sitio, a plan of providing sites with minimal housing and urban facilities to be developed in stages, with savings and auto-construction by the residents, with official supervision. The Frei government stands out in Latin America in the degree of its commitment to finding housing solutions for the poor. An indicator of its unparalleled accomplishments in this regard is the fact that in 1969 the last of the squatter settlements were almost totally eradicated from metropolitan Santiago, their residents having found a location in an Operación Sitio settlement.

Nonetheless, there is evidence that the program is too static and too isolated in conception to be adequate to popular needs even in the near run. With urbanward migration, natural increase, and metropolitan redevelopment, the number of poor people seeking the minimal Operación Sitio solution is growing faster than even a reformist government's capacity to acquire land in the urban periphery, urbanize it minimally, and place the needy on it.

As a consequence both of the growing need for low-cost housing solutions and growing governmental involvement in the field, demand on government has also increased. The failure of the program to keep pace has provided the Marxist-coalition opposition parties with an opportunity. Major Santiago-area land invasions by the poor with FRAP help have increased from a rate of single large-scale seizures in 1947, 1957, 1960, 1961, 1965 to two in 1967, and six major and several minor ones in 1969; more are likely in the near future. A premium is now put on organization of those seeking a housing solution from the government. The administrative process involves application for Operación Sitio (or other plans) and the opening of an account in a state bank in which quotas are deposited, representing savings for the future place in a program (Sanders, 1969). The leaders of the committees of homeless help organize the necessary documentation and quota purchases and negotiate the arrangements with the bureaucracy.

The number of committees organized to push Operación Sitio demands is very large. Some attain their goals sooner, some later, and some are delayed through what seems to the members to be political reasons.

In any case, the Communist Party and its newspaper have increasingly emphasized organization of this social sector, particularly those who encounter substantial delay in resolving housing problems. The Party has only in 1969 been able to develop municipalitywide associations of homeless in the poorer metropolitan districts, plus a metropoliswide association organized under the auspices of the major labor central, itself dominated by the FRAP. For the first time a march of the homeless of greater Santiago was carried out by the coordinating body.

THE HISTORY OF A FRAP-AFFILIATED LOS SIN CASA COMMITTEE[7]

The first step is the drawing together of an aggregate of people needing housing. Little is presently known about this stage, but it involves many grass-roots leaders and participants who have no previous public political experience. Increasingly these are becoming amalgamated into a municipalitywide organization sometimes representing several thousand families. A preliminary meeting with a representative of the housing ministry will result in a general plan, but at any stage the committee experiences irritating delay contacting the "right" bureaucrat. At some point the ministry will make a commitment to find a particular solution within a roughly specified period, assuming the fulfillment of a set of conditions by the committee. There follows a protracted period of committee activity to promote quota purchases by the membership and the maintenance of collective spirits for the difficult savings effort. From time to time, the committee returns to the officials with a progress statement in an effort to nail down the official commitment. Frequently it is difficult to locate the same official, who is "at a meeting" or "out of town," so that the committee leadership composed of working people lose pay and time. To minimize this loss, their delegations may include a congressional deputy known for his support of the homeless. If even this fails, visits are made to the communist newspaper or a popular daily that tends to make brief reports on such situations. Finally a specific set of commitments will be won.

When the committee comes close to meeting its end of the bargain, it again tries to meet with the officials to make certain that due dates will be respected. If doubt arises on this score, frequently the case, given the overextendedness of the ministry, variations in marshaling pressure are tried. In some cases marches are held to dramatize the plight of the homeless and evasion by the officials. Frustration wells up when deadlines are missed, as the cramped and desperate situation of the people is felt to be no longer supportable. A massive sit-in in the ministry has been used to stop all other official business and virtually force the bureaucracy to deal with the committee. At that juncture, feelings are so high that any anger or disdain shown by officials toward the people vastly increases the intensity of the demand, and the legitimacy felt by the committee is reinforced by their sense of broken promises. Sometimes such forced meetings reveal that the minister or key official is crucially misinformed about the nature of the "deal" between the committee and the government; in fact he may even assume from internal reports that the problem has already been resolved. Such revealed slippage also reinforces the insistence of the committee. Further steps may include a history of the process in the communist or socialist paper, an attempt to petition the president directly, and the threat to invade land as others before have done.

With the passage of a reset deadline, and after intensified organization and even a rehearsal by the committee, a land invasion occurs, usually in the early morning hours. Materials sufficient to throw up a scanty shelter are carried near the site, and at a signal the homeless rush onto the field, raise flimsy tents, each with a national flag; then comes the tactical squad of the police. Warnings will be given, entreaties made by the committee leadership together with supporting FRAP congressmen and local FRAP councilmen. Frequently the police attack to dislodge the invaders. Infrequently a few deaths occur, but there are always the injured, and tear gas, stones thrown, and a melee to create scenes of horror for the children. The people will be pushed off to the side of the road and allowed to stay there temporarily. Sometimes the matter will be resolved within days, but months may also be consumed in negotiations. The insalubrious conditions of the camps bring sickness; in winter up to forty children have died of broncopneumonia contracted in the soaking, frigid postinvasion conditions. Food, scarce under normal circumstances, becomes even more so for lack of money and access to markets. This is made worse by the upsurge of unemployment, resulting from job loss as the men stay on the invasion site to protect their families.

In these crisis circumstances, the high level of organization achieved by the FRAP-supported (particularly the communist) committees shows itself from the outset. Discipline in the camps is tight, liquor barred, vigilance-committee assignments made, a central headquarters with loudspeaker is set up, a provisional first-aid station established; if necessary, a common soup kitchen is started. The Communist Youth is mobilized to collect food, money, and medicine. Frequently from the first day on, folksingers affiliated with the party (sometimes Chile's finest) arrive to perform, showing outside solidarity with the "heroic" invaders. Almost immediately the camp will take a symbolically potent name, such as either the date of the invasion, or a martyr created during the first invasion stages. The establishment newspapers that ignore the situation of the poor will publish stories emphasizing the breakdown of law and order and communist manipulation of the ignorant poor.

In the end, the determination and obvious suffering of the people, their large numbers, the relative legitimacy of their claims, and the furor created by FRAP congressmen and municipal officials encourage the government to negotiate a solution. After additional time necessary to minimally urbanize a site, the invasion group is transferred to their land.

The extreme hostility generated by the confrontation means that subsequent governmental assistance in urbanization will be extremely slow in coming. Nonetheless there are recent signs that the morale generated by the successful invasion and the high level of organization of the invaders carry over to animate community development efforts (Portes, 1969). Their success becomes legend in communist efforts to organize other los sin casa committees. Leaders who have arisen in the course of the experience become officers of new, more inclusive organizations of the poor. Folk singers, recruited from the invasion-established community, perform before other committees and propagate an obvious example. The community is cited repeatedly in political propaganda, which reinforces its pride and augments the meaning of its experience. Partisan follow-up may include summer vacation art classes for the children where they draw pictures of the actual invasion scenes, and parks may be established in adjoining grounds named for heroes of international communism, such as Ho Chi Minh, to promote a broader radical perspective. Foreign delegates may visit the site. Within months come announcements that so many hundred new recruits have joined the Juventud Comunista from the new invasion community. Though some undoubtedly were oriented in this direction prior to the committee experience, newspaper interviews suggest that many others were politicized and radicalized in the course of it.

CONCLUSION

This description of political processes involving the homeless does not demonstrate but provides evidence in accord with the proposition that adults, previously inexperienced and uninvolved in politics, learn to engage in and sustain complex political demand-making under certain circumstances. The most important of these seem to be a sense of acute needs, a perception of a strategy of action adequate to meeting the needs, and the availability of an organization to channel the action.

This reading of the experience of the homeless should be related to a recent study of political participation based on large-scale comparative-survey analysis. One of its principal findings was that people involved in organizations may be politically active even though they lack certain psychological bases (such as efficacy, informedness, attentiveness) frequently considered requisites of political action. Regarding organizations, the authors (Nie et al., 1969: 813) suggest that:

> Apparently mobilization opens direct lines to participation, or provides attitudinal resources relevant to specific problems only. There might be, for instance, group-initiated political discussion, group-organized contacts with political authorities, or group-related political information relevant to a specific issue.

This seems to fit the experience of many of the homeless extremely well. Moreover, the cynicism with attendant disinterest expressed by many of the poor toward government and politics seems a function of the general lack of relevance of the latter to their needs, despite much propaganda to the contrary. But when a political organizational channel exists through which an acute need can be met, then apparently information is generated, consumed, and carefully planned political efforts are made, even over a relatively long period of time.

That organizations meeting the needs of the poor are relatively rare does not excuse the tendency on the part of social science to ignore their efficacy as agencies of rapid, intense political socialization. It is precisely through the development of such organizations that the lack of political involvement of the poor may be most efficiently overcome. In fact, the analysis of survey data collected from former invader groups that had had a roughly similar experience to those of the los sin casa indicates that such organizations, after demonstrating their efficacy in meeting an acute need, proceed generally to politicize the people. The high level of politicization reflected by the FRAP invader groups is such evidence.

We have tended to look at the process of political socialization in too unstructured a fashion, the primary model being one of gradual learning by children of political information, attitudes, values, and practices through the family and school, with the national environment as a diffuse factor. The poor or lower-status sectors do tend to be politically socialized to passive, relatively apolitical roles in a polity such as ours. But increasingly numerous revolutionary cases call attention to the extraordinary amount of mass political socialization of adults, as well as children, through organizations designed to produce new men by channeling their behavior.

A consideration of recent Cuban experience shows that an extremely high level of political participation can be mobilized and sustained among the previously apolitical poor when organizations are created and officially promoted for this purpose, and when governmental policies are so directed to the needs of the poor that support is generated. The Cuban government has gone a long way toward providing security for the poor regarding housing (low rents), food, medical care, and employment. Furthermore, schooling has been vastly extended, and more than anywhere else in Latin America, equal opportunity has become the basis for recruitment to postprimary education. From all accounts I have seen, the degree of support of this government by the poor, especially the youth, has been high, as evidenced by volunteer labor, participation in the militia or Committees of Defense of the Revolution, attendance at political events, obedience to the law and to the spirit of the law, and community development efforts, even discounting substantially for political and peer-group pressures (Fagen, 1969; Hochschild, 1969; Yglesias, 1968; Trans-action, 1969; Zeitlin, 1967).

The previously mentioned comparative study of social structure and political participation finds that economic development promotes political participation by increasing the proportion of middle- and upper-class people in the society, because upper status promotes attitudinal resources and learning situations fostering participation. But even in economically developed nations, "the majority of citizens do not participate very actively in politics and do not have the attitudinal resources which lead to citizen control of public policies" (Nie et al., 1969: 825-826). Since, as previously cited, political participation also flows importantly from organization, participation can be fostered:

> It appears that the richness and complexity of organizational life might be altered somewhat independently of economic development. Deliberate governmental policies, for instance, can increase the number of citizens who are politically active. Mobilization parties ... are one example of how this might happen [Nie et al., 1969: 826].

The further point is necessary that such deliberate participation-expanding policies may be designed to elicit participation in politically relevant activities that directly promote economic development. The multiple organized efforts of the Cuban government to recruit the citizens, including many of the young and poor, for volunteer labor such as cane-cutting or carrying literacy campaigns to the uneducated throughout the island, or the agricultural development of the Isle of Pines, are designed both to promote economic development and to transform the political culture through involvement in collective activities.

This study has focused on the way in which political organizations can relate to needs to politicize socioeconomically deprived people. In the study of political socialization, those of low status are typically found to be, and generally considered to be, low in politicization, without analyzing the power structural factors that result in this condition. By inference, the low politicization of the poor, especially in the United States, is considered normal. To the extent our analysis is valid, it suggests that the politicization of the poor, or anyone else, depends crucially on organization relevant to their needs. Where such organization does not exist, the politicization of the poor will be low. Where it can function, their politicization will be higher, and where it functions with official sanction and can define as politicial and strive to meet a wide range of needs, their politicization will be even higher. And as the Cuban case indicates, such participation can be promoted so as to bear vitally on the work of economic development.

NOTES

1. For further description of the study and background on these communitites and their urbanization context, see Goldrich et al. (1967).
2. Equivalent data distinguishing between original invaders and latecomers were unfortunately not collected in 3 de Mayo.
3. The scoring method refines that used on the general scale in that it not only segregates local indicators, but reveals intensity of local involvement rather than its mere existence.
4. This item was used to form part of the Political Efficacy Scale, a component of the overall Politicization Scale, but since we are dealing here only with the activist politicization type, no particular bias intrudes when the data are analyzed regarding area of political problem that the poblador could present to one or another governmental office.
5. In neither case is this disparity a function of the primarily FRAP control of the labor unions, which might be assumed to promote an economic problem orientation among poblador workers. There is no difference in proportion of union members among activists of Christian democratic or FRAP affiliation.
6. A more precise test of these propositions through natural experiments to control levels of politicization among the homeless prior to and after the demand process culminating in invasion will be, unfortunately, extremely difficult to carry out. Such a research strategy almost necessarily means a panel study, in turn requiring identification of subjects by the researcher. Since invasion is obviously illegal, and secrecy critical to its success, and since such social-research techniques are unfamiliar and such social science stigmatized by the left as a United States plot, the obstacles appear enormous.
7. The observations on which this section is based were made during relatively brief field work periods in 1965 and 1967, and an eighteen-month period in 1968-1969. During the last period, depth interviews were carried out with a small number of leaders of past and present los sin casa committees, some of whom participated in invasions. In addition, newspaper files were compiled, periodic visits made to invasion sites, meetings of los sin casa committees were attended, and interviews were held with party and ministry officials concerned with the problem. Data were collected from at least some participants affiliated with all of the relevant political parties. The description generally is drawn from the experience of six major invasions in the past two and a half years.

REFERENCES

ABRAMS, C. (1966) Man's Struggle for Shelter in an Urbanizing World. Cambridge, Mass. MIT Press.
FAGEN, R. (1969) The Transformation of Political Culture in Cuba. Stanford: Stanford Univ. Press.
GOLDRICH, D. et al., (1967) "The political integration of lower-class urban settlements in Chile and Peru." Studies in Comparative International Development 3: 1-22.
GIUSTI, J. (1968) "Rasgos organizativos en el poblador marginal urbano latinoamericano." Revista Mexicana de Sociología 30 (Enero-Marzo): 53-77.
GURRIERI, A. (1966) "Situacion y perspectivas de la juventud en una poblacion urbana popular." Revista Mexicana de Sociología 28 (Julio-Septiembre): 571-602.
HOCHSCHILD, A. (1969) "Communism on Treasure Island: Cuba's Isle of Pines." Liberation 14 (December): 15-21.
INSTITUTO DE INVESTIGACIONES ECONOMICAS. (1965) Estudio Socioeconómico de una Barriada. Lima: Universidad Nacional Mayor de San Marcos.
LANGTON, K. (1969) Political Socialization. New York: Oxford Univ. Press.
MANGIN, W. (1967) "Latin American squatter settlements: a problem and a solution." Latin American Research Rev. 2 (Summer): 65-98.
NIE, N., B. G. POWELL, Jr., and K. PREWITT. (1969) "Social structure and political participation: developmental relationships, II." Amer. Pol. Sci. Rev. 63 (September): 808-832.
PORTES, A. (1969) Cuatro Poblaciones: Informe Preliminar sobre Situación y Aspiraciones de Grupos Marginados en el Gran Santiago. Santiago: Programa Sociología del Desarrollo de la Universidad de Wisconsin.
SANDERS, T. (1969) "Juan Pérez buys a house." American Universities Field Staff Reports, West Coast South America Series 16, 2: 1-17.
Trans-action (1969) "Cuba: ten years after." (special issue) 6 (April).
YGLESIAS, J. (1968) In the Fist of the Revolution. New York: Pantheon.
ZEITLIN, MAURICE. (1967) Revolutionary Politics and the Cuban Working Class. Princeton: Princeton Univ. Press.

APPENDIX

CONSTRUCTION OF THE POLITICIZATION SCALE

The scale is based on four subscales, the first three of which are simply aggregative. High, medium, and low scores were made on each subscale.

Salience. This is measured by an item on interest in what government does, two open-ended opinion items in which the expression of an opinion is considered an indicator of political salience, and an open item about anything that has happened in politics the respondent considers to have affected his life very much.

Sense of Personal Political Efficacy. This is based on two items, one of which concerns whether one's role is only as a passive recipient of government action or an active agent that can influence government action; and an open item about what one might do to get government to act or cease acting in a given way.

Access. Channels of access into decision-making processes are indicated by affiliation with a political party, membership in unions and the local association of the community, and knowing someone who can help one make use of government programs.

Participation. Unlike the previous subscales, participation is not merely aggregative. High participation is defined as having discussed politics in at least two contexts (described below), plus having directly tried to get government to do something, or having attended political meetings, or having taken part in demonstrations. Medium participation is defined as either discussion in two contexts, or at least one of the more concerted activities, while low participation is defined as having done neither of those. The discussion contexts are defined as at least occasional discussion of politics with family, or friends, or coworkers, or politicians, or, a separate item, any discussion of the Dominican Revolution, a major international event that occurred just prior to the survey.

SCHOOL EXPERIENCES AND POLITICAL SOCIALIZATION

A Study of Tanzanian Secondary School Students

KENNETH PREWITT
GEORGE VON DER MUHLL
and DAVID COURT

KENNETH PREWITT *is Associate Professor of Political Science at the University of Chicago. His publications include* Political Socialization *(co-author) and* The Recruitment of Political Leaders, *as well as contributions to scholarly journals.* GEORGE VON DER MUHLL *is now teaching at the University of California, Santa Cruz. He is currently engaged in a larger study of the impact of educational experience on the formation of citizenship values in three East-African countries.* DAVID COURT *is a graduate of Cambridge University and former volunteer teacher in Tanzania. He is currently at the Stanford International Development Education Center where he is completing his Ph.D.; his thesis investigates the effect of different schooling experiences on social learning in Tanzania.*

Two differing theoretical perspectives have characterized the study of political socialization. One perspective begins with the nation-state, or some aspect thereof, as the phenomenon to be explained. Evidenced about children's views as well as how children come to hold these views is introduced as possible explanatory data. When Easton and Dennis (1969: 4) link political socialization findings to the analysis of why political systems persist, they provide an instructive example of this theoretical perspective.[1] The second and by far the more frequently encountered perspective begins with the political beliefs of children as the phenomenon to be explained. The analyst then introduces evidence about the socialization process, socialization agencies, and so forth. When Hess and Torney

---

AUTHORS' NOTE: *This paper is part of a larger study entitled "Education and Citizenship in East Africa." The Rockefeller Foundation provided funds for the*

(1967) set out to explain the "development of political attitudes in children," they illustrate this theoretical perspective. Although the same data can be used to either purpose and a single study can incorporate both perspectives, the two perspectives do differ. The first perspective deals with the system question of what defines politics in a nation; the second, with the question of what accounts for the political views and beliefs of citizens.

The present analysis falls within the range of issues and problems raised by the second perspective, though we pay homage to the broader questions in the conclusions. Our analysis rests on the paradigm conventionally used in studies of political socialization. A child undergoes various socialization experiences and, because of this, acquires political norms or in some cases replaces one set of norms with another. Since political socialization experiences vary with time, and time with age, it is possible to speak of the political socialization process. The child ages; as he does, he is under the influence of a varying sequence of socialization agencies, is exposed to varying politically relevant stimuli, is experiencing varying types of political events, and so forth. It is because of these influences, exposures, and experiences that he comes to think and act according to a citizen role. He acquires a "political self."

However simple this paradigm appears, its application in empirical research has proven a difficult task. Three conceptual ambiguities have beset this enterprise. We shall note these ambiguities before applying the paradigm to data collected from Tanzanian students.

EMPIRICAL DIFFICULTIES IN APPLYING THE POLITICAL SOCIALIZATION PARADIGM

(1) Age as an independent variable. Frequently in political socialization studies the age of the child (or his grade level in school) is introduced as the independent variable; what the child believes about politics is considered the dependent variable. Research findings follow a typical pattern: The attachment of younger children to the nation is based on positive evaluation of authority figures, whereas the attachment of older

---

collection of the data and the Stanford International Development Education Center provided support for data preparation from a grant from the U.S. Office of Education. The Center for the Comparative Study of Political Development at the University of Chicago provided funds for the preparation of this paper. A general description of the study as well as related papers can be found in Kenneth Prewitt (ed.), Education and Political Values: Essays About East Africa *(Nairobi: East African Publishing House, 1971).*

children is more likely to be based on identification with highly valued symbols. This is a useful and even important finding. But phrased in terms of younger and older, it is stripped of much of its theoretical potency. We can see why this is so by looking more carefully in the research paradigm at age.

When we relate aging to children's orientations toward politics, we intend to suggest at least two things. As children age, they characteristically experience certain intrinsic changes—changes in their capacity to process information about the world, in their ability to cope with emotional stress, and so on. Thus we expect that older children will have a richer fund of human experience on which to draw when interpreting political events, that they will show a greater propensity to formulate abstract rules of conduct, that they will exhibit greater sensitivity to the reactions of their peers. But as children age they are also characteristically subjected to predictable changes in the terms on which others interact with them. They are held more accountable for their actions, their judgment is taken more seriously, they are given greater freedom to seek out new associates and try out new experiences.

These changes correlate highly with age, but none is conceptually identical with the chronological demarcations of the life cycle that we refer to as age. And it is these changes, not the chronological lapse in time itself, that are relevant to the student of political socialization. We can see this point clearly if we think of cases where age is artificially speeded up or retarded for the individual. A child who shows early signs of a high IQ may, for purposes of political socialization, be regarded as older than his chronological peers. Alternatively, variations in cultural patterns or certain dramatically deviant experiences—e.g., the plight of an orphaned refugee child during a war—may age a child for purposes of analysis. Although it may seem desirable to separate conceptually the factor of age from IQ or maturational experiences, it is hard to think of the relevance to socialization studies of the chronological phenomenon apart from these correlates.[2]

Studies of political socialization which show older and younger children to differ in their political norms are somewhat misleading. Since the correlates of aging are left out of the design, theorizing activity tends to concentrate on age itself as the critical experience. But age is clearly an inappropriate independent variable; it is simply another way of saying, through time. And the research paradigm already assumes that political norms vary with age. Thus using age as the independent variable is tautological—it simply restates the initial assumptions.

(2) Age as a surrogate variable. There are political socialization studies in which age is used not as the independent variable but as a surrogate for changing socialization experiences, the true independent variable. Again, the format of research findings follows a typical pattern: The older child, being less under the influence of parental authority and more influenced by peer relations than the younger child, tends to view rules as conventions commonly agreed upon rather than as arbitrary injunctions handed down from above. The empirical assertion is that the manner in which authority structures are experienced affects what children come to believe about the nature and source of rules. Of theoretical interest is the observation that an important political belief varies according to the relative salience of competing socialization agents. That the salience of these agents varies with the age of the child is of some interest, but the finding could be stated without reference to older and younger and still be of theoretical interest. It could not be written without reference to parental authority and peer relations and still be of much use for purposes of theorizing.

What is absent in political socialization research are designs which vary age and hold experiences constant, or vary experiences and hold age constant. The appropriate comparison, of course, is to compare the same individual as he undergoes different socialization experiences. Thus we might determine whether his political norms change as he leaves the nuclear family and is exposed to the peer culture of the school. Any research strategy short of this will understandably weaken attempts at theory construction. What makes the age of the child important is that he cannot be simultaneously undergoing contrasting socialization experiences; thus to compare his norms under varying conditions implies to compare him at different ages.

It seems to us that, in the absence of longitudinal data, the strategy which approximates the ideal socialization study is to compare children who have clearly different experiences. In the illustration cited here, for instance, it might be instructive to compare younger children being raised in a permissive orphanage with older children being raised by very strict parents. If it were found that the younger children had the value thought to be associated with peer influence and the older children had the value thought to be associated with parental influence, theorizing would be given a great boost.

(3) Traits as independent variable. The point can be underscored by considering one additional application of the variables in the political

socialization paradigm. We might label this the trait approach. A characteristic of the individual child is said to be an independent variable. Typical statements are: High-IQ children differ from low-IQ children in their sense of efficacy; black children differ from white children in their level of political cynicism; girls differ from boys in their amount of political knowledge. If this approach were depicted with reference to the variables in the paradigm, it would look as follows:

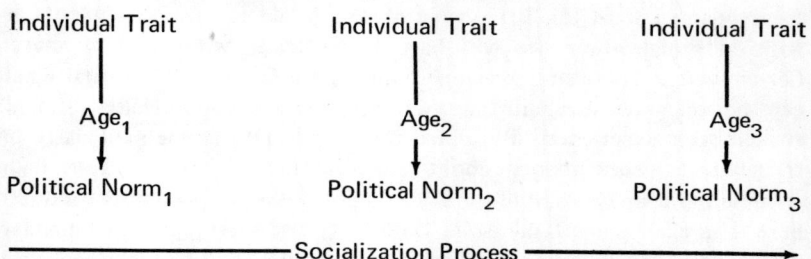

Individual Trait   Individual Trait   Individual Trait

Age_1 Age_2 Age_3

Political Norm$_1$ Political Norm$_2$ Political Norm$_3$

―――――――――― Socialization Process ――――――――――→

Seen diagramatically, the difficulty with this approach is immediately apparent. The so-called independent variable is not a variable. Sex, IQ level, race, and similar traits are constants for the individual. They vary only across the population taken as a whole. But to understand political socialization as a process necessarily implies that that which is to account for the development of the political self be a variable, one which varies for the child as he matures. Introducing a constant such as sex as the independent variable is simply a back-door method of making age the actual independent variable. What is being implied is that a child experiences his IQ or his race or his sex differently at different ages, and thus there are changes in his political orientations. We might expect, for instance, that five-year-old whites and blacks will have very divergent perspectives. This is a way of saying that a child experiences the color of his skin differently at different ages. We suppose that this converts the constant into a variable, but it does not make for very powerful social theory. Of greater relevance to theory are findings which reveal how socialization experiences differ for black and white children of different ages.

POLITICAL SOCIALIZATION EXPERIENCES: AN ALTERNATIVE TO AGE

A clear conclusion emerges from this sketch of a few difficulties which beset the empirical study of political socialization. We have studies with dependent variables but no independent variables. What is offered the reader of the political socialization literature are attitude surveys of children wherein it is demonstrated that the age of the child helps to order the dependent items. These surveys do not actually make the political socialization research paradigm operational. What is needed are research strategies identifying the manner in which differing socialization experiences lead to differences in political norms. This is difficult to do with survey data, but as this is the type of data available to most students of political socialization, we will have to make do with what we have. Certainly it is important that longitudinal data be collected so that what can be seen to vary, for a given child, are his politically relevant socialization experiences. But since we are as guilty as the next party in trying to squeeze theory about a developmental process from data collected at a single point in time, we do not bother to preach that sermon here. The challenging task, as we see it, is to use survey data in a manner which does permit some reasonable sound application of the political socialization paradigm. A preliminary start in that direction will occupy our efforts in the remainder of the paper.

RELIGION, SCHOOLING, AND POLITICAL SOCIALIZATION IN TANZANIA

Survey data collected from Tanzanian secondary-school students permit us to compare political views of students who have had contrasting school experiences. The general notion is a simple one. The student's schooling either has been consonant with whatever dispositions are associated with his earliest religious instruction, and thus should reinforce those dispositions, or it has not, in which case it should attenuate whatever dispositions are associated with his religion. We will be doing two things simultaneously: first, attempting to make operational a research strategy which stresses differing experiences, and second, exploring a hypothesis about school environments as reinforcing experiences.

Our analysis does not intend to make the student's religion a variable. For the individual, religion is a constant. What can vary are the school experiences which might affect how persons of the same religion view the political world and their place in it. This point may become somewhat lost in the following pages as we introduce data about Protestants and Catholics. But the purpose of using students from different religions is simply to allow independent tests of the hypothesis. Whatever we have to

say about differences from one religion to
central task.[3]

To underscore this point it need onl
considerations other than religion could
instance, students who spent their pres
classified according to whether they at
urban schools, or some mixture. It co
dispositions associated with being rural were acc
attending only rural schools, and so forth. To add to this analysis,
who were raised in urban areas would permit another test of the hypothesis and not necessarily lead to statements about differences between rural and urban youth.

For the students of Tanzania, ministers of religion were among the earliest agents of socialization encountered outside the family. Furthermore, formal association with a church was either a cause or a condition of initial entry to school. A student's religion is thus an important aspect of his personal identity. All but one percent of our sample identify themselves as Catholics, Protestants, or Muslims. That this attachment is more than a nominal label of convenience adopted for the sake of a school place is shown by the pattern of responses to items of our questionnaire, which indicate strength of religious affiliation. Eighty-seven percent of our respondents regard marriage to someone of their own religion as very important or important. This proportion contrasts with 58% and 49% who attach a comparable degree of importance to partners of similar tribe and educational level respectively. In a consistent vein, when students were asked to report the extent of their trust for a variety of significant others, the degree of trust for religious leaders exceeded that for all other persons except fathers. When faced with the difficult task of choosing between the importance of nation, religion, and tribe for their lives 56% of the students ranked religion first, 41% ranked the nation first, and the remaining 3% chose tribe first.

That religion is an important aspect of self-identity for the Tanzanian student is easily understood. As Oginga-Odinga (1967: 63) points out in his autobiography, "The missions dominated African education. The government, by neglecting to provide state schools, left the field to the various denominations, which presided over their schools and congregations as though over small empires." Missionaries were the bearers of the modernizing values and responsible for the development of formal education. Today all schools are responsible to the national government, but in organization and general tone strongly reflect the nature of their

ency. In our sample, schools founded by a religious society are
almost exclusively by students of the corresponding religion,
s the government schools are heterogeneous in religious compo-
n. This is shown in Table 1.

There is little doubt that the mission and government schools represent different types of experience for the student exposed to them. In the mission school a student is surrounded by peers and teachers of his own religion. The regular communal rituals of religious observance in which he participates are familiar to him, and he is selectively exposed in his daily school life to a pervasive and consistent church perspective.

Contrasting experiences affect the student whose education occurs in a government school. Here the student encounters a pattern of life which is basically secular in tone and which lacks the monolithic perspective which is symbolized in the mission schools by the awesome presence of the school chapel. Institutional religious observances are perfunctory or nonexistent and school assemblies less frequent than in mission school. Students are exposed to a variety of normative expectations amid a religiously heterogeneous student body, and are in contact with a staff who are characterized by their diversity of ideological viewpoint.

This pattern of the founding agency and school composition means that the school experiences of a given individual may progressively reinforce

TABLE 1
TYPE OF PRIMARY AND SECONDARY SCHOOL ATTENDED BY STUDENTS OF DIFFERING RELIGIONS[a]
(in percentages)

Student's Religion	Sponsoring Agency of Secondary School			Sponsoring Agency of Primary School			
	Catholic (330)	Protestant (109)	Government (451)	Catholic (389)	Protestant (292)	Government (198)	Muslim (24)
Catholic	87	10	29	92	2	33	0
Protestant	10	67	42	3	84	28	0
Muslim	2	22	29	5	14	38	100
Total	99[b]	99	99	100	100	99	100

a. It should be emphasized that we are using data from a purposive sample, which excludes day school students, female students, and non-Africans. Thus the above proportions do not represent the distribution of all types of students in differing schools of Tanzania. They do, however, approximate the correct distribution of students in all-male boarding schools, since these schools are drawn from a random sample of all schools in Tanzania.

b. Due to rounding error.

the perspective of his religious identity, or contrast with it, according to whether or not his primary and secondary schooling occur in mission schools of his own religion.[4] For example, a Catholic whose primary and secondary education occur in Catholic mission schools will have a more reinforcing set of school experiences than one who attends government schools. Inconsistency may be first met at the primary or secondary level, or be reversed, in the case of a student who attends a government primary school and proceeds to a mission school of his own religion.[5] The four types of cumulative schooling experiences possible for, as an example, a Catholic student, are:

Primary School	Secondary School
Catholic	Catholic
Catholic	Government
Government	Catholic
Government	Government

Logically many other patterns are possible, as, for instance, the Catholic attending a Protestant school in some combination with either a government or Catholic school. Instances of pattern other than those used in this paper are so infrequent that they have not been included in the analysis (see Table 1).

The sample. The data on which this paper is based are drawn from a larger national sample of secondary schools in Tanzania.[6] Because we do not intend here to make generalizations to the national population, our subsample is purposive. The object of selection was to match students, as far as possible, on all characteristics of their school experience except the dimensions of interest, i.e., founding agency and religious composition. Thus the respondents are drawn from the same Form 4 level of secondary school. The eight schools which provide the students of our subsample are alike in sex and racial composition and in their social and geographical isolation. They are all boarding schools, situated at some distance from the capital city, and are attended solely by African males. These male students are almost all from a background of subsistence farming and are of comparable age.[7] The schools vary mainly in terms of founding agency— Catholic, Protestant, and government—and cater to individuals of three types of religious affiliation: Protestant, Catholic, and Muslim.

ANALYSIS

It was previously noted that the Tanzanian students take seriously their religious affiliation. We see in Table 2 that the extent to which religion as an individual trait is reinforced by school experiences does affect the strength of religious commitment. The importance of religion is greatest for those students who have attended religious primary and secondary schools, and this pattern holds for both the Protestants and the Catholics. This table indicates two other matters of interest. The interreligious differences are not great; in fact, the relative weight assigned to religion is nearly the same for Catholics (59%) and Protestants (55%). Secondly, for students of both religions, the major differences appear to occur between those who are in a religious secondary school and those who are in a government secondary school. These are important tendencies, and we will keep them in mind as we examine responses to other questions.

A question allowing the students to indicate how important they consider religious instruction in schools forms the basis for Table 3. Again, it is evident from looking at the totals that Catholics and Protestants do not differ regarding the importance of religious instruction. But intrareligious differences do appear and in a pattern consistent with that reported in Table 2. Students who have spent their school years solely within church-related schools give less secular answers than do those students who have been in government schools. Again it appears to be secondary experience more than primary experience which contributes to this result.

TABLE 2
PROPORTION OF STUDENTS WHO CONSIDER RELIGION OF MORE IMPORTANCE THAN NATION, BY INDIVIDUAL RELIGION AND PATTERN OF REINFORCEMENT[a]

Pattern of Reinforcement	Catholics %	n	Protestants %	n	Totals %	n
Reinforcement at primary and secondary stages	64	(207)	57	(75)	62	(282)
Reinforcement at secondary stage only	64	(34)	57	(21)	62	(55)
Reinforcement at primary stage only	43	(96)	52	(134)	48	(230)
No reinforcement	53	(17)	38	(26)	44	(43)
Totals	59	(345)	54	(249)		

a. Students were asked to choose which was more important: nation or religion, nation or tribe, tribe or religion. The proportions reported in this table derive from the students whose rank order was religion-nation-tribe (46% of the total sample), or religion-tribe-nation (10% of the total sample).

TABLE 3
PROPORTION OF STUDENTS WHO STRESS RELIGIOUS INSTRUCTION IN THE SCHOOL, BY INDIVIDUAL RELIGION AND PATTERN OF REINFORCEMENT[a]

	Individual Religion					
	Catholics		Protestants		Totals	
Pattern of Reinforcement	%	n	%	n	%	n
Reinforcement at primary and secondary stages	44	(233)	50	(84)	45	(317)
Reinforcement at secondary stage only	37	(41)	52	(21)	42	(62)
Reinforcement at primary stage only	29	(102)	37	(138)	34	(240)
No reinforcement	33	(18)	34	(29)	34	(47)
Totals	39	(394)	42	(272)		

a. Students were asked to rank order the importance of five different aspects of a hypothetical school curriculum. Proportions here reported are those students which ranked religious instruction as first, second, or third in importance. Of the total sample, 40% ranked religious instruction as third or higher.

In Table 4 we turn attention from items directly related to a secular-religious continuum to an issue not necessarily linked at all to religion. The pattern recorded in tables 2 and 3 is repeated, the dependent variable now being whether progress, individual or national, can proceed easily without government assistance. To note first the intrareligious differences, the students whose schooling has been reinforcing—which in the present instance means to be isolated from secular influences—tend to show a lower sense of personal efficacy than do students whose schooling has occurred in government schools. The same pattern appears in the second part of the table; government direction of social improvement is seen as more important by those who have only attended religious schools than by those in government schools. And, as with the previous tables, the secondary-schooling experience differentiates more sharply than the primary-schooling experience.

One additional item is relevant. Table 5 records data pertinent to the overall appraisal these students voice about Tanzania. They were first asked what they were most proud of in their country, and they then were asked if there was anything in Tanzania that they were not proud of. In general, few students took this opportunity to voice complaints, and the uncritical appraisal was slightly more prevalent among Protestant than Catholic students. However, once again the schooling experience itself is related to how students answered. The more critical students are those who, in this instance, are isolated from the influence of government schools. Thus, for instance, while all of the Protestants who have always

TABLE 4
EXTENT TO WHICH STUDENT BELIEVES INDIVIDUAL AND SOCIAL PROGRESS IS DEPENDENT ON GOVERNMENT DIRECTION (two items), BY INDIVIDUAL RELIGION AND PATTERN OF REINFORCEMENT

	Individual Religion					
	Catholics		Protestants		Totals	
Pattern of Reinforcement	%	n	%	n	%	n

1. Proportion who agree that an individual can do little to improve his lot without governmental assistance.

Reinforcement at primary and secondary stages	53	(238)	41	(85)	50	(323)
Reinforcement at secondary stage only	39	(43)	40	(22)	40	(65)
Reinforcement at primary stage only	32	(105)	32	(142)	32	(247)
No reinforcement	28	(18)	31	(29)	30	(47)
Totals	45	(404)	36	(278)		

2. Proportion who agree that the people of Tanzania can do little to improve their country without governmental direction.

Reinforcement at primary and secondary stages	52	(237)	58	(86)	54	(323)
Reinforcement at secondary stage only	58	(43)	59	(22)	58	(65)
Reinforcement at primary stage only	44	(106)	38	(140)	41	(246)
No reinforcement	33	(18)	30	(30)	31	(48)
Totals	50	(404)	45	(278)		

attended Protestant schools cite something they are not proud of, more than one-fifth of Protestants in government schools say there is nothing they dislike about Tanzania.

We will elaborate on the general findings later, but at this point we can provide a summary statement. The central finding is revealed by an overall interpretation of Tables 2 through 5: the average difference between Catholics and Protestants is six percentage points; the average difference between those students whose schooling has been reinforcing and those whose schooling has not is three times this size. We tentatively conclude that (with respect to dependent variables used here) the schooling experience is more important for how these students orient themselves toward religion and society than are their differing religious beliefs—this despite the fact that religious affiliation is an important part of the self-identity of Tanzanian students.

Table 6, however, bids us to be cautious with respect to hasty general conclusions. Students were asked to weigh the immediate attainment of

TABLE 5
PROPORTION OF STUDENTS WHO HAVE NO CRITICISMS TO RECORD ABOUT TANZANIA, BY INDIVIDUAL RELIGION AND THE PATTERN OF REINFORCEMENT[a]

	Individual Religion					
	Catholics		Protestants		Totals	
Pattern of Reinforcement	%	n	%	n	%	n
Reinforcement at primary and secondary stages	6	(174)	0	(38)	4	(247)
Reinforcement at secondary stage only	9	(23)	0	(12)	6	(35)
Reinforcement at primary stage only	25	(85)	28	(120)	26	(205)
No reinforcement	21	(14)	22	(23)	22	(37)
Totals	13	(296)	20	(193)		

a. Students were asked if there were things about Tanzania which they were not proud of. Proportions reported here indicate students who said there was nothing they were not proud of. The smaller n indicates the large number of students who did not answer this question, a response pattern partly attributable to the fact that the question was followed by an open-ended item (they were to record what they were not proud of); and fewer students answered open-ended items.

individual and familial ends against submission to rules designed to advance diffuse collective goals. On this measure, the different schooling experiences had considerable effect on Protestant students, but very little on Catholics. The reasons for these interreligious differences cannot be explored here. Table 6 is included to emphasize that the independent variable used here does not relate to all political values, nor should we

TABLE 6
PROPORTION OF STUDENTS WHO SUPPORT GOVERNMENT EVEN IF PERSONAL SACRIFICE IS INVOLVED, BY INDIVIDUAL RELIGION AND PATTERN OF REINFORCEMENT[a]

	Individual Religion					
	Catholics		Protestants		Totals	
Pattern of Reinforcement	%	n	%	n	%	n
Reinforcement at primary and secondary stages	48	(233)	74	(83)	54	(316)
Reinforcement at secondary stage only	44	(43)	73	(22)	54	(65)
Reinforcement at primary stage only	48	(101)	54	(138)	52	(239)
No reinforcement	56	(18)	62	(29)	59	(47)
Totals	48	(395)	63	(272)		

a. Students were asked which person helps Tanzania more, the person who pays school fees and then cannot pay taxes, or the person who pays taxes and then cannot pay school fees. Proportions here recorded are those students who said taxes should be paid.

expect it to. However, it is the task of another report to identify the range of political values affected by the reinforcement pattern.

INTERPRETATIONS

In this report we have attempted to operationalize a research paradigm, and in so doing, to explore a hypothesis about the effect of different schooling experiences influencing views of Tanzanian secondary-school students. Before assessing the value of the methodological strategy and the significance of the findings, we should reemphasize one matter. The research design permitted us to hold the age of the student constant while varying his experiences. More specifically, we have not compared students of different age levels, an approach common in political socialization studies limited to survey data. Rather we have taken students of the same grade levels and have classified them according to differences in their schooling experiences. The socialization experience investigated refers to the degree of consonanced between a student's religion and characteristics of his school environment. This variable is chosen because we know religion to be an important part of the self-identity of Tanzanian students, and because of the juxtaposition of government and mission schools within the educational system of Tanzania.

The evidence indicates that differences in political views among the students are related to differences in schooling experiences. Intrareligious differences can be as great or greater than interreligious differences. This general finding can now be elaborated by inquiring into the relative impact of the different experiences. This is accomplished most directly by amalgamating the several tables into a single composite score.

Table 7 presents data pertinent to understanding the relative impact of primary and secondary experiences. The table should be read as follows: The first half holds secondary schooling constant and compares students who differ in their primary schooling; the second half reverses this by holding primary schooling constant and varying the secondary school attended.

Although differences occur at both the primary and secondary levels, the secondary-school experience has the greater impact. This is true of both Protestant and Catholic students. The presence or absence of reinforcement in their school experience is more significantly related to their social attitudes if it occurs at the secondary rather than at the primary level. We discuss this below, but we should not allow this general finding to lead us to ignore the fact that primary schooling has some effect. Students of the same religion attending the same secondary schools do have somewhat different political and social orientations if they attended different types of primary schools. Further confirmation that primary schooling does make a difference is suggested by the responses of Muslim students. Since there are no Muslim secondary schools, it was not possible to include them in the main analysis. However, we have compared Muslims who attended Muslim primary schools with Muslims who did not. The average difference on the items used in this paper is twelve percent, with Muslims who did not attend Muslim primary school consistently resembling the modal pattern associated with other students who attend only government schools. We cannot explore these data in detail here, but they do confirm that the primary experience can affect outlook independently of secondary schooling.

The degree of difference recorded in Table 7 reflects the differing impact of a mission- as opposed to a government-school experience. Reasons for these differences almost certainly lie in the different type of environment which government and mission schools provide for their members at both the primary and secondary level. These differences, already described, include the contrast between homogeneity and heterogeneity in religious composition of student body and staff, the contrast between a generally sacred and a secular tone to school life, and the contrast between a pervasive and an infrequent religious-ritual life. Before

TABLE 7
MEAN PERCENTAGE DIFFERENCES IN POLITICAL VALUES BETWEEN DIFFERENT GROUPS OF STUDENTS CLASSIFIED ACCORDING TO PATTERN OF SCHOOLING EXPERIENCES

Holding Secondary Schooling Constant	%
Catholics attending Catholic secondary but different primary schools	6
Catholics attending government secondary but different primary schools	6
Protestants attending Protestant secondary but different primary schools	4
Protestants attending government secondary but different primary schools	5

Holding Primary Schooling Constant	%
Catholics attending Catholic primary but different secondary schools	14
Catholics attending government primary but different secondary schools	12
Protestants attending Protestant primary but different secondary schools	16
Protestants attending government primary but different secondary schools	15

discussing these differences further, however, we should consider an alternative interpretation of Table 7.

The possibility that self-selection processes account for our findings cannot be overlooked. The argument would be that individuals whose religious attachments are strongest are more likely to attend mission schools than government ones. If this is the case, some of the reported variance in our criterion variables should be attributed not so much to the content of different patterns of experience undergone by students as to the different personal qualities which they bring to those experiences.

While some confounding of selection and contextual factors cannot entirely be ruled out, the nature of the selection process in Tanzania, and the salience of religion for most students, makes the above interpretation implausible. We have earlier shown that nearly all the students of our sample consider religion to be an important part of their identity. Further, in a situation of restricted opportunity, selection for secondary education is on the basis of regional quotas from a national examination. In the allocation of an individual to a particular mission secondary school, his religious label is usually taken into account, so that Protestants are not normally assigned to a Catholic mission school and vice versa. Within this general condition students are normally allocated to the school which is closest to their home. The selection process takes no account of the relative strength of an individual's religious affiliation. In short, we have no reason to suppose that students who enter government schools possess different qualities than their mission-school peers. (Self-selection might, however, explain the Muslim differences noted above.)

There are, on the other hand, differences between primary and secondary schools which, when considered in the context of political socialization theory, might explain the relatively greater impact of the secondary school. One difference of importance has to do with the residential nature of secondary schools and a second has to do with the unique character of secondary schools.

The secondary education of our respondents is a residential experience, whereas their primary education occurred in day schools. Levine (1966) has pointed to the geographical isolation and monopoly of student time as reasons for the socializing potential of the African boarding school. A growing body of research literature lends support to this view. Wheeler (1966: 55), for example, suggests that "the intensity of a socializing experience is probably related to the degree of separation; for separated settings are able to reduce potentially conflicting influence." The typical isolated location and internal structures of the East African boarding school invite analogy with the total institution as discussed by Goffman (1961). The central features of his model can be listed summarily:

(1) All aspects of life are conducted in the same place and under the same single authority.
(2) Each phase of daily activity is carried out in the company of others and all are treated alike.
(3) All phases are tightly scheduled.
(4) All activities are part of a general plan for fulfilling official aims.
(5) There is a clear division between staff and inmates.

If the above features are truly those which contribute to the socializing power of an institution, they are much more evident in the secondary-boarding schools than in the primary-day schools of East Africa. As they are common, in varying degree, to each type of secondary school, they could help to account for the distinctive effect of each type on its members (Weinberg, 1967).

An alternative explanation for the relatively greater socializing impact of the secondary-school experiences stresses the different relationship of primary and secondary schools to their social context. The general notion is that the socializing power of a school, or class of schools, over its members depends on its ability to facilitate their entry to elite status (Meyer, 1968). In Tanzania, where educational opportunity is very limited, secondary schools of whatever type, because of their unique control over the avenues of social mobility, have a derivative power to socialize students in their own image. From the student's viewpoint, the overwhelming fact that he has been singled out for a secondary education leads him to value and see as legitimate whatever norms and practices happen to accompany the particular type of schooling experience which serves to guarantee his future.[8]

Both of the explanations which have been advanced for the findings in Table 7 are no more than speculations which invite empirical refinement. The findings themselves, however, do increase confidence in the utility of investigating the schooling experience in terms relevant to socialization theory.

CONCLUSION

In two respects this paper represents an early step in our data analysis. First, we are just beginning to explore the data for their substantive meaning, especially for what we can learn about political orientations and their implications for the development of a new nation through studying the political views and learning experiences of that nation's schoolchildren. The more inclusive research goal we have in mind is to identify how the political culture of an African nation takes shape through its political socialization processes during the immediate postindependence years. The substantive interest in this paper has, of course, been much narrower in scope, dealing only with a subgroup of the total student sample and with only a few of the many variables available. Nevertheless, we are able to report two substantive findings: The tenacity of religious identity in orienting the views of young Tanzanians lingers on despite the insistence in that nation on a nationalistic political culture; moreover, the extent to which religious identities shape political and social views is affected by the schooling experiences of the young. From a theoretical point of view these are rewarding findings. It appears that the distinctive characteristics of Tanzania's unfolding political culture are indeed related to patterns of socialization experiences associated with the schools.

This paper represents an early step in our analysis in a methodological sense as well. It is not easy to theorize about the way in which the political socialization process occurs when the data available are neither collected over time nor contain detailed materials on the process itself. We experimented in this paper with one method of making statements about socialization processes from survey data, and are heartened by the outcome. We deliberately refrained from comparing students of differing ages, for reasons outlined in the first section of the paper. We also refrained from speculating at length about youth who differ in their political views because they are members of different subgroups in that nation, a practice we earlier called the trait approach in socialization research. Instead, we determined to see if different sets of socializing experiences might have predictable relationships to how the students of Tanzania orient themselves to the nation during its early years. We found this to be the case, and we can now suggest some of the broader implications which might follow from the findings.

The finding that a distinctive type of schooling experience influences, in a predictable way, the social views of Tanzanian students has dual significance: first, in relation to research about the effects of formal education; and secondly, with reference to current educational policy in Tanzania.

Much previous research, following a trait approach, has demonstrated that educational attainment is a major predictor of an individual's political attitudes. These studies have usefully identified a category of experience—namely, formal education—which is crucial in the formation of civic norms. Yet in using years of education or grade level as the major independent variable, such studies treat education as a homogeneous and incremental experience. They have not gone on to specify the critically determining elements and patterns of that experience, or the conditions under which these elements influence the development of civic norms for particular classes of individuals. Dennis (1968: 109) refers to this problem when he states that "schools may show high variance in their capacity to shape the political outlook of their charges. The size of the school, its quality, its curriculum, its location, its social composition, and the like may all serve to dampen or increase its relative effect."

Our purpose has been to investigate one influential pattern of school experience. To be sure, earlier studies have investigated the sources of variance in the impact of schools on students, but they have centered mainly on the American college. A recent review (Newcomb and Feldman, 1969) of this research concludes that very few of these studies have managed to identify elements of impact which are distinguishable from selection factors. While we hesitate at this stage of our analysis to proclaim an addition to the few, we are heartened at the possibilities our analysis suggests. The relatively great insulation of the Tanzanian boarding school from competing agencies of socialization, together with the essentially impersonal and nondiscretionary character of the intake process, gives grounds for attributing variances in the civic orientations of boarding-school students to the varying qualities of the schools themselves. The convenience of the matching process employed in our analysis confirms this view that the control conditions inherent in the Tanzanian setting make it possible to investigate crucial school experiences more precisely there than within the American educational system.

A further implication of our study relates to national policy. Most African leaders view their schools as major agencies of national development. Schools are expected to produce students who graduate with technical competence, but also with dispositions relevant to the demands of social and political development. There is consensus that the colonial system of education is inappropriate for these purposes. There is less agreement on what characteristics of school structure and content can be manipulated to produce new orientations. This uncertainty exists precisely because so few empirical relationships have been established between specific characteristics of schooling experience and identifiable student norms.

Nevertheless, Tanzania is unique among African nations in the extent to which it has self-consciously sought to adapt the educational system it inherited at independence to the goals of the postcolonial leadership. Its government is currently engaged in an extensive effort to restructure both the educational curriculum and the organization of school life in the hope of producing a deeper commitment to the new social order.[9] The significance of this effort is not to be judged by the number of students involved. Barely five percent of the appropriate age group enter secondary school, and attrition reduces still further the percentage of those who graduate. Yet secondary schools remain virtually the exclusive channels of recruitment to positions of influence in Tanzania. With certification by educational authorities still an almost indispensable passport to participation in the higher levels of the government, and with entrance into the government closely coupled to the completion of higher education, the schools appear as a strategic and potentially manipulable variable conditioning the civic commitments of Tanzania's future political elite. Belief that the schools can be used in this manner is given voice in a recent statement by Tanzania's Minister of National Education (Mgonja, 1968):

> Thus steadily our pupils are being orientated to our own mode of life and our own set of values, with the emphasis on service to the community.... The youth we take into our schools today will after some years return worthy to take their places in their society—and not only that—they must enrich that society and breathe new life into it, instill in it the desire for purposeful development and provide the necessary unified sense of direction for the whole country.

Our findings do indeed offer some empirical support for President Nyerere's (1967) recent declaration that the source of the social dispositions of Tanzania's students is to be found in the character of their schools. The differences in orientation produced by varied reinforcement patterns imply that differing educational experiences contribute in distinctive and critical respects to the formation of differing civic values. What is much less clear is whether these differences are directly traceable to consciously created differences in the character of the schools. It has not been our purpose in this article to stress the substantive nature of variations in the dependent-variable items, but we should emphasize here that the fact of patterned variation is in itself no warrant for concluding that the intended messages of each school agency reach their pupils unaltered. Curriculum content and teacher attitudes have been assigned primacy of place in Tanzanian discussions of educational reform; yet our findings suggest that, if anything, the more elusive elements in the social ambiance of the schools may be the more determinative of student outlooks. Our analysis so far permits no conclusion more sweeping than that missionaries and secular-minded educational officials have been alike correct in supposing that the question of school agency has not been a trivial one.

NOTES

1. Easton and Dennis (1969: 4) write: "Even though we begin by talking about children and will extensively analyze data about them, this book is really about political systems. It addresses itself to one major condition—socialization—that contributes to the capacity of a political system to persist in a world either of stability or change."

2. We appreciate that previous political socialization studies have found politically related cognitive development to be linked, for American children, to specific ages. Greenstein (1965) reports that there is a large advance in children's understanding of political roles between ages 11 and 12—the period of life when the child begins to acquire the capacity for formal operations. (See also Gallatin and Adelson, this volume.) Such findings, in part, challenge the point of view we are developing. However, the interesting variable is not the age of the child so much as his capacity for formal thought.

3. It follows that the patterns we intend to emphasize in our analysis emerge primarily from reading our tables downward through varying combinations of school experiences, rather than horizontally, from Catholic to Protestant.

4. Because each mission school predominantly admits students of its respective faith while government schools have religiously heterogeneous student bodies, the denominational or secular character of these schools must be viewed as the joint product of peer-group influences and the institutional ambiance created by the administrative staff. The current stage of our analysis does not permit us to distinguish these effects. Our references to the socializing experience of attending the schools of a designated agency must thus be taken to cover a multiplicity of forces presumed to work in the same direction.

5. We are overlooking the denominational and national differences between missionary agencies within each religious group. In terms of consistency of reinforcement for the student, these differences are less important than those between the groups and the government schools. It should be noted, however, that our use of reinforcement and inconsistency (or, more accurately but awkwardly, nonreinforcement) refers to the degree of consonance between the formal objectives of the school agencies in question and the formal religious affiliation of the individual respondent. Whether attendance at a mission school consonant with an individual student's affiliation actually reinforces his denominational commitments any more than attendance at government schools is a specific empirical issue beyond the scope of this article.

6. The Education and Citizenship study includes data from Kenya, Uganda, and Tanzania. Primary- and secondary-school students are being studied. Primary- and secondary-school students in Tanzania, and thus a brief note about that part of the sample will suffice. In May, 1966, the Tanzanian Ministry of Education list of secondary schools showed sixty schools with a Form 4 level, and fifteen Higher Schools with a Form 6. Beginning with a randomly chosen school, we selected every sixth school with a Form 4 on the Ministry list, and every third school with a Form 6. This procedure yielded ten secondary and five higher schools. This sample exhibited the full range of school types, and came very close to matching the expected proportion of schools in such categories as rural-urban, day-boarding, coed-single sex, Protestant-Catholic-government, and so forth. To permit more refined analysis in a few schools, we added to our sample the Form 2 and Form 4 classes in our Form 6 schools where such forms were part of the same school. All students within any given form were given a self-administered questionnaire. Every school in the sample was visited, and cooperation was excellent. A total of 1,821 Form 2, Form 4, and Form 6 students completed the questionnaire.

7. Although there is some variation in the age of the Form 4 students in our sample, the degree of variation is not sufficient to vitiate our objective of holding age constant while investigating other determinants of differing orientations.

8. This thesis is developed at greater length by Prewitt, "University Students in Uganda: Selection Patterns and Political Style," in Hanna [ed.] (1970). The competition for school places is sufficiently intense and absorbs so much of the energy and thinking of students that the norms associated with student status tend to be more fully adopted than in school systems less competitive and where the risks of failure are less severe.

9. For an early report on the rationale and the constraints underlying these efforts, see G. Von der Muhll, "Education, Citizenship, and Social Revolution in Tanzania," in Prewitt [ed.] (1970).

REFERENCES

DENNIS, J. (1968) "Major problems of political socialization research." Midwest J. of Pol. Sci. 12 (February): 85-114.
EASTON, D. and J. DENNIS (1969) Children in the Political System: Origins of Legitimacy. New York: McGraw-Hill.
GREENSTEIN, F. (1965) Children and Politics. New Haven: Yale Univ. Press.
GOFFMAN, E. (1961) "The characteristics of total institutions," in A. Etzioni (ed.) Complex Organizations: A Sociological Reader. New York: Holt, Rinehart & Winston.
HESS, R. D. and J. V. TORNEY (1967) The Development of Political Attitudes in Children. Chicago: Aldine.
INHELDER, B. and J. PIAGET (1958) The Growth of Logical Thinking from Childhood to Adolescence. New York: Basic Books.
LEVINE, R. A. (1966) "Political socialization and culture change," in Clifford Geertz (ed.) Old Societies and New States. New York: Free Press.
MEYER, J. W. (1968) "The charter: conditions of diffuse socialization in schools." Unpublished. Stanford University.

MGONJA, C. Y. (1968) "Revolution in education." Report by the Minister of Education in the Republic Day Supplement of the Tanzania Standard. 7 (December).

NEWCOMB, T. M. and K. FELDMAN (1969) The Impact of Colleges Upon Their Students. New York: Jacob Losey.

OGINGA-ODINGA (1967) Not Yet Uhuru. New York: Hill & Wang.

PREWITT, K. (1971) "University students in Uganda: selection patterns and political style," in William Hanna (ed.) University Students in Politics: New York: Basic Books.

--- (1970) Education and Political Values: Essays About East Africa. Nairobi: East African Publishing House.

WEINBERG, I. (1967) The English Public Schools. New York: Atherton Press.

WHEELER, S. (1966) "The structure of formally organized socialization settings," in O. Brim and S. Wheeler (eds.) Socialization After Childhood. New York: John Wiley.

VON DER MUHLL, G. (1970) "Education, citizenship, and social revolution," in Kenneth Prewitt (ed.) Education and Political Values: Essays About East Africa. Nairobi: East African Publishing House.

INDIVIDUAL RIGHTS AND THE PUBLIC GOOD

A Cross-National Study of Adolescents

JUDITH GALLATIN and JOSEPH ADELSON

JUDITH GALLATIN *is Assistant Professor of Psychology at Eastern Michigan University, Her interests include adolescent growth and change.* JOSEPH ADELSON *is Professor of Psychology at the University of Michigan, where he is also associated with the Psychological Clinic. Among his several publications is* The Adolescent Experience *(with Elizabeth Douvan).*

The recent acceleration of research on political socialization has made it evident that decisive advances in political understanding are achieved during the adolescent years. To some considerable degree this growth stems from a more general advance in cognitive capacity, in particular the shift from concrete to formal operations (Inhelder and Piaget, 1958). In part, it derives from hte adolescent's change in self-definition: prior to adolescence the youngster sees himself as entirely subject to the moral authority of the family and of social institutions; in adolescence he begins to view himself as morally autonomous and as a participant in the larger events of the community.

These developmental shifts influence the adolescent's level of political awareness and sensibility. Research findings now suggest that the prepubescent youngster enjoys only a dim grasp of abstract political concepts. His view of political institutions is generally personalized, centering upon an awareness of public officials, such as the president or mayor, but with little understanding of their roles, or indeed of the structure and mechanisms of government (Greenstein, 1965; Hess and Torney, 1967). Adelson and O'Neil (1966) report that before the age of fifteen the child has no effective comprehension of such abstract ideas as "law" and "government," and tends to discuss social policy by gener-

---

AUTHORS' NOTE: *Funds for the data collection were provided by grants to the second author from the H. H. Rackham Fund of the University of Michigan and from the Social Science Research Council.*

alizing from the familiar domains of personal experience—that is, in terms of those rules and concepts of equity which he has experienced in the family, at play, and in the schoolroom. Furthermore, views of law and government tend, in the early years of adolescence, to be authoritarian and moralistic, with an excessive emphasis on "keeping people in line"; only later in adolescence do we find youngsters emphasizing the positive functions of law and adopting a relativistic and pragmatic perspective on political events (Adelson et al., 1969).

This report will center upon a traditional issue in political philosophy: the interaction between the public good and individual rights. Fundamental to western political thought is the idea of social contract, wherein the citizen cedes certain rights and freedoms to the state in the understanding that the yielding of these enables the government authority to provide for the common good. The state in turn must set and abide by certain limits upon its hegemony over the citizen; in particular, it must not encroach upon certain freedoms except when their exercise clearly endangers the public welfare. In liberal democracies the task of achieving the proper balance between the public good and individual autonomy is at the heart of many and perhaps most political conflicts. Do the collective benefits achieved by a proposed law or policy warrant an infringement upon the citizen's property, freedom, or welfare?

The intention of this paper is to examine changes in the apprehension of these issues during the course of adolescence. The research strategy is both developmental and cross-national. Are there significant shifts in the perception of these problems from the preadolescent to the late-adolescent years? To what degree are these changes a function of maturation itself, and in what way, if any, are they influenced by differences in social experience? Specifically do youngsters in different countries with varying political traditions have different developmental patterns? We will compare matched samples of adolescents, from eleven through eighteen years of age, in three western countries—the United States, Great Britain, and West Germany.

METHOD

The interview. The data were obtained by an interview schedule, which proposed the following hypothesis: A thousand people, dissatisfied with their government, moved to a Pacific island to form a new society. Once there, they confronted the task of establishing a political order. The schedule then posed questions ranging over a wide array of topics—the nature of law and government, political forms and functions, the sources of crime and the strategy of punishment, utopianism, and so on. The questions were open-ended for the most part and semiprojective. In complexity they ranged from the simple open-ended type (e.g., on the purpose of government or law) to complex sequences of questions which considered in some detail specific dilemmas the society faced (e.g., a series of items on the control of cigarette smoking.

The interviews were conducted in school, tape-recorded, and transcribed verbatim. They were generally completed in sixty to ninety minutes. Interviewers were graduate students in psychology, all with some previous experience in clinical interviewing.

The sample. In all, 330 boys and girls between and ages of 10 and 18 were interviewed. Four grade levels were sampled: the fifth, seventh, ninth and twelfth (average ages, respectively, 11, 13, 15, and 18). There were 120 American subjects drawn from a Midwestern suburb, 120 British youngsters from the London suburbs, and 90 German adolescents from Hamburg and environs. For each age level 30 subjects were chosen, half of them boys, and half of them girls, two-thirds of average intelligence (95-110) and one-third of superior intelligence (125 plus). Due to fund limitations, German fifth-graders were not interviewed; therefore, cross-national comparisons to be reported here do not include that grade for any of the national sample. To sum up, each grade level and each national sample is also matched for sex and intelligence.

With respect to social status, the American and German samples are roughly comparable—largely middle class, with the American having a somewhat higher number of upper-middle-class cases. The British sample is overall somewhat lower in social status, containing a larger number of subjects from working- and lower-middle-class backgrounds. However, the findings we will report were analyzed by social class without significant differences emerging. Furthermore, analyses by sex and IQ also failed to find differences. Consequently, this paper will focus upon differences associated with age and national origin.

Reliability. Ten percent of the total sample of interviews were selected randomly to establish reliability. Intercoder agreement for this sampling ranged from eighty to ninety percent.

RESULTS

The Public Good

How does the adolescent attain the idea of the public good? The following two items from the interview schedule allow us to observe the development of this concept.

> Question 18. Another law was suggested which required all children to be vaccinated against smallpox and polio. What would be the purpose of that law?
>
> Question 14. Some people suggested a law which would require children to go to school until they were sixteen years old. What would be the purpose of such a law?

The findings reported in Table 1 demonstrate the emergence of a sociocentric orientation in the later years of adolescence. The purpose of a vaccination law is seen, prior to the age of fifteen, to be primarily the protection of the individual citizen; at fifteen and over, the communal necessities—that is, the public good—is felt to justify the law.

The response to the education question, shown in Table 2, is considerably more complicated—not surprisingly, in view of the more complex functions served by education. We find, as we did earlier, that with increasing age there is a heightened awareness that compulsory public education aims to benefit the community as a whole. At the same time, other trends are discernible as a function of increasing age. Younger adolescents are more likely to offer a simple-minded approbation of education, a view which reflects their tendency to acquiesce without much apparent thought to the arrangements and values that the world proposes.

TABLE 1
AGE DIFFERENCES IN ARGUMENTS FOR VACCINATION LAW

	By Age			
	11	13	15	18
1. Preserve the health of individuals.	66	69	36	30
2. Community survival.	34	31	64	70
Total	100% (59)	100% (90)	100% (87)	100% (88)

x^2 = 39.467 (3), p $<$ .001

Younger subjects are also more likely to stress the narrow economic advantages of education, an emphasis which seems personalistic. However, we find with increasing age a sharp increase in another more subtle and more abstract form of personalism: the tendency to see education as enhancing self-actualization, the rounding and deepening of the self. All in all, it appears that there is no simple progression from a personalized to a sociocentric view of education; the earlier forms of personalism, which stress economic gain, diminish and are succeeded by a sense of the more complex benefits of education. Simultaneously there is an increased comprehension of the public good by the sample as a whole.

National differences. We found no significant differences among the national groups in regard to the purpose of vaccination. In Table 3, however, on the functions of education, we see some striking national variations. The American sample stresses its benefits to the community—a theme which will be evident in later findings as well. The American youngsters are oriented to the public purposes of education, to its function in assuring the progress and survival of the community—an orientation which Barry (1965) has termed "aggregative utility." The British subjects more frequently see education in terms of its direct benefits to the individual, regarding it as a means by which people can advance economically and vocationally. They seem to entertain a "fair shares for all" philosophy—in Barry's terminology they stress "distributive utility." The German sample are more inclined to concern them-

TABLE 2
AGE DIFFERENCES IN ARGUMENTS FOR
EDUCATION LAW

	By Age			
	11	13	15	18
1. Unreflective: end in itself.	44	38	28	21
2. Increase economic opportunities.	33	39	32	17
3. Preparation for life: self-actualization.	00	07	13	18
4. Benefit to community: progress, survival, etc.	23	16	27	44
Total	100% (54)	100% (89)	100% (84)	100% (88)

$x^2 = 38.08$ (9), $p < .001$

selves with the less tangible benefits of education. It is seen either as an end in itself or as a means for preparing the individual for life. Relatively speaking, they are less concerned either with the community's benefit or with the economic advantages of education.

Sharpening the Issue

The two items we have reviewed so far are fairly straightforward, requiring only that the subjects state the purpose of a particular policy. These items were, in fact, largely preparatory for the two following questions, which draw attention more explicitly to the delicate course a government must steer in dealing with conflicts between the general good and the interests of specific groups.

Question 20. There was a small group of people on the island who were members of a religion which was opposed to vaccination. They said that their religious beliefs disapproved of vaccination. What would you do in a case like that?

Question 24. A lot of the money that was collected by taxes was to go to the public-school system on the island. But the people who did not have children thought it was unfair that they would have to pay taxes to support a school system. What do you think of that argument?

Developmental results. The responses to the vaccination item (Table 4) make it apparent that what changes over time is not so much the solution proposed, but the form of reasoning which supports the solution. About the same proportion of younger and older subjects are in favor of having

TABLE 3
NATIONAL DIFFERENCES IN ARGUMENTS FOR EDUCATION LAW

	By Country		
	American	British	German
1. Unreflective: end in itself.	26	20	42
2. Increase economic opportunities.	26	42	18
3. Preparation for life: self-actualization.	4	9	25
4. Benefit to community: progress, survival, etc.	44	29	15
Total	100% (89)	100% (85)	100% (84)

$x^2 = 43.71$ (6), $p < .001$

the dissenting religious group vaccinated (combining categories 1, 4, and 5, sixty percent of the eleven- to thirteen-year-olds, and the same proportion of fifteen- and eighteen-year-olds argue for vaccination). We have, however, some important changes in the principles adduced to argue the position.

The older children are much less likely to declare that the recalcitrant sect should be treated harshly and somewhat more likely to justify vaccination on the grounds that it will protect the community as a whole. If, on the other hand, they favor waiving the requirement for conscientious objectors, they are less likely to assume an air of indifferent laissez faire and more likely to argue for religious tolerance than the younger children. In short, there is increasing appeal to political and humanitarian principles and less allegiance to more punitive and moralistic postures. The older adolescent is less inclined to force choices on individuals; he is also less inclined to become vindictive and simply leave them to their fate when they dissent. As in the education item in the previous section (see Table 2), commitment to community goals and increased respect for human dignity appear to be concurrent developments.

The question of whether childless adults should pay school taxes draws a slightly different pattern of responses. Again a majority of both younger

TABLE 4
AGE DIFFERENCES IN OPINIONS AS TO WHETHER CONSCIENTIOUS OBJECTORS SHOULD BE VACCINATED

	By Age			
	11	13	15	18
1. Coercion: religious group should be forced, exiled, or segregated.	38	30	27	14
2. Religious tolerance: group should be free to worship as it pleases.	4	23	23	31
3. Laissez faire: group should be left to its fate.	31	23	17	11
4. Community welfare: group should be vaccinated for public welfare.	2	5	10	15
5. Persuasion: group should be reasoned with.	25	19	23	29
Total	100% (56)	100% (78)	100% (86)	100% (81)

$x^2 = 36.52$ (12), p $<.001$

and older subjects favor the policy proposed by the government. But in this case a larger number of older subjects comes out in support of the public-school system (if we combine categories 1, 2, and 3 in Table 5, 85% of the fifteen- and eighteen-year-olds vs. 64% of the eleven- and thirteen-year-olds would have childless adults do their part). In addition to this quantitative difference, there are marked differences in arguments. The eleven- or thirteen-year-old is likely to feel that childless adults should pay school taxes "because it's the law" or "because they might have children some day." In other words, he tries to justify the law on the grounds either that people should obey the existing political order or that they will derive some direct benefit from education. If both of these justifications fail, he is likely to take a narrowly self-interested view of the matter: people shouldn't have to pay for what they don't use. The fifteen- and eighteen-year-olds, by contrast, demonstrate far more awareness of community goals. Whatever the interests of a private individual, these older subjects seem to be saying he has a stake in the community as a whole. Since the community will benefit by maintaining a high standard of education, even those citizens without children should help to support the

TABLE 5
AGE DIFFERENCES IN OPINIONS ON WHETHER CHILDLESS ADULTS SHOULD PAY SCHOOL TAXES

	By Age			
	11	13	15	18
1. Uncritical compliance: childless adults should pay; direct benefit.	24	31	11	7
2. Injustice, inequity: childless adults would be breaking the rules by not paying.	17	21	22	16
3. Community welfare: childless adults will benefit indirectly from having educated citizenry.	17	18	48	66
4. Private interest, lack of utility: childless adults should not have to pay for what they do not use, or should pay less.	42	30	19	11
Total	100% (58)	100% (84)	100% (88)	100% (88)

$x^2 = 68.21$ (9), $p < .001$

schools. It should be emphasized that the older subjects are not necessarily less "pragmatic" than the younger ones. It is rather that the older adolescents seem to consider the utility of a particular policy for the group as a whole rather than figure it on an individual basis. In short, what we see once again is a progression from distributive to aggregative utility.

Equally important, a comparison of the responses to questions 20 and 24 suggests an increasing differentiation of political issues with increasing age. Comparatively few of the older subjects argue that the community as a whole will benefit from having conscientious objectors vaccinated, though a large number of them employ this argument to justify the taxation of childless adults. Both questions pose a conflict between the individual's insistence on self-determination (negative rights) and the government's attempt to provide its citizens with a basic minimum (positive rights). But in one case a substantial number of older subjects support the prerogatives of the individual, and in the other an even more substantial number back the government. As the adolescent matures, he seems also to become aware that the resolution of conflicts between individual and state depends both upon the policy advanced by the state and the nature of the objections offered by the individual. Though they might possibly demoralize the community by their example, a religious group which refuses to be vaccinated does not pose any major threat to the rest of the community—provided, of course, that the rest of the community is vaccinated. On the other hand, a group of childless adults who refuse to support the public-school system may impair the progress of the community as a whole. The older subjects seem to have public issues like these in mind, while the focus of the younger subjects is largely private.

National differences. We find some marked national differences in response to these items, especially so with regard to the compulsory vaccination question. (Table 6). The American sample in particular is distinctive in its disavowal of a coercive solution and its emphasis on religious tolerance. For a substantial number (nearly half) of the subjects, the principle of religious freedom overrides the otherwise desirable goal of universal vaccination. Among those in the sample who propose compulsory vaccination, the Americans, here as elsewhere, are somewhat more likely to make explicit the needs of the community.

The German youngsters provide a sharp contrast. They are far less likely than the Americans to argue for religious tolerance (44% to 11%). Instead, a substantial number—70% in all—propose that pressure be brought to bear on the dissenters, either through coercion or by reasoning and persuasion.

Relative to the others, the British steer a middle course. They are more likely than the Americans and less likely than the Germans to advocate coercion; they propose religious tolerance more often than the Germans, but less often than the Americans do. What is perhaps most striking about them is their relatively greater tendency to adopt a laissez faire solution: If people want to take chances, they seem to be saying, that is their own business.

On the question of whether the childless should pay school taxes, national differences, though present, are less prominent (Table 7). The Americans, again, are the most ready to adduce the issue of the public good, arguing that the interests of all are served by public education. The British once more are relatively more partial to private interests, arguing more frequently that the childless ought not to pay for what they do not use; there is perhaps a trace of the laissez faire sentiment here that we have noted before in their responses. The Germans are more inclined to justify general taxing policy by a stress upon rules: it would be unjust for the childless to break the rules by refusing to pay.

The interaction of age and country. On the vaccination controversy, the developmental pattern varies among the national samples (Table 8). The strongest changes are visible among the American subjects: for most categories we see a fairly linear increase or decline. The preference for coercion of the religious group decreases from thirty-seven to three

TABLE 6
NATIONAL DIFFERENCES IN OPINIONS AS TO WHETHER CONSCIENTIOUS OBJECTORS SHOULD BE VACCINATED

	Country		
	American	British	German
1. Coercion: religious group should be forced, exiled or segregated.	14	25	31
2. Religious tolerance: group should be free to worship as it pleases.	44	21	11
3. Laissez faire: group should be left to its fate.	9	27	15
4. Community welfare: group should be vaccinated for public welfare.	15	10	6
5. Persuasion: group should be reasoned with.	18	17	36
Total	100% (81)	100% (84)	100% (80)

$x^2 = 46.49$ (8), $p < .001$

percent over the age range; there is also a distinct decline in laissez faire sentiment. These choices are replaced by a substantial increase in the statement of religious tolerance and by increase in emphasis on the public welfare. The American developmental pattern is deeply etched: considerations of religious freedom and, to a lesser degree, of the public good (nearly invisible at eleven years of age), rise until they dominate the views of the eighteen-year-olds.

But developmental changes are not nearly so evident for either the British or German samples. The British show some marked changes at the eighteen-year-old level—a decline in the coercive choice, and an increase in the public-good category; otherwise, there is no marked developmental pattern. The German youngsters show some decline in their use of the laissez faire alternative and some increase, at eighteen, in their emphasis on persuasion. Yet in neither case do the developmental shifts as a whole attain conventional levels of statistical significance, despite the inflation of chi-square.

On the issue of public education (Table 9), there is much greater similarity among the national samples. In all three groups support of the community is dominant by the age of eighteen; that is, the subjects agree that taxpayers without children should support the public schools because they will achieve indirect benefits through the progress and survival of society. There are, however, some distinct national tendencies. The idea of the public good is, once again, more marked in the American sample than

TABLE 7
NATIONAL DIFFERENCES IN OPINIONS AS TO WHETHER CHILDLESS ADULTS SHOULD PAY SCHOOL TAXES

	Country		
	American	British	German
1. Uncritical compliance: childless adults should pay; direct benefit.	13	17	18
2. Injustice; inequity: childless would be breaking the rules by not paying.	15	15	29
3. Community welfare: childless adults will benefit indirectly from having educated citizenry.	55	40	38
4. Private interest; lack of utility: childless adults should not have to pay for what they do not use, or should pay less.	17	28	15
Total	100% (86)	100% (87)	100% (87)

$x^2 = 12.84$ (6), $p < .05$

TABLE 8
OPINIONS AS TO WHETHER CONSCIENTIOUS OBJECTORS SHOULD BE VACCINATED: AGE BY COUNTRY FINDINGS

	By Age Within Country			
	11	13	15	18
American				
1. Coercion	37	25	14	3
2. Religious tolerance	3	38	41	54
3. Laissez faire	33	16	7	3
4. Community welfare	0	9	17	18
5. Persuasion	27	12	21	21
Total	100% (30)	100% (24)	100% (29)	100% (28)
British				
1. Coercion	43	27	38	10
2. Religious tolerance	3	27	10	28
3. Laissez faire	29	27	31	24
4. Community welfare	3	4	3	21
5. Persuasion	21	15	17	17
Total	100% (28)	100% (26)	100% (29)	100% (29)
German				
1. Coercion	—	36	29	29
2. Religious tolerance	—	7	18	9
3. Laissez faire	—	25	14	9
4. Community welfare	—	3	11	4
5. Persuasion	—	29	29	54
Total		100% (28)	100% (28)	100% (24)

America[a]: $X^2 = 36.94$ (12), p .001; England[b]: $X^2 = 19.68$ (12), p .10; Germany[c]: $X^2 = 10.31$ (8), NS

a., b. and c. Chi-square restrictions are not met; therefore, the chi square is considerably inflated. (The expected frequency in more than 20% of the cells is less than 5.)

in the others; nearly nine-tenths of the American eighteen-year-olds so respond. Another national nuance is the strong emphasis on the private interest among the eleven- and thirteen-year-old British subjects. Younger subjects are in general more likely to emphasize the direct benefits of public policy, and we have already seen that the British tend to emphasize distributive utility. Hence, we may be observing here the interaction between a developmental trend and a more general national attitude.

DISCUSSION

With regard to developmental patterns, this study supports earlier findings (Adelson and O'Neil, 1966) on the growth in adolescence of a

TABLE 9
OPINIONS AS TO WHETHER CHILDLESS ADULTS SHOULD PAY SCHOOL TAXES: AGE BY COUNTRY FINDINGS

	By Age Within Country			
	11	13	15	18
American				
1. Compliance: direct benefit	36	26	10	3
2. Injustice; inequity	14	37	10	0
3. Community welfare	29	15	57	89
4. Private interest ascendant	21	22	23	8
Total	100% (28)	100% (27)	100% (30)	100% (29)
British				
1. Compliance: direct benefit	15	29	10	13
2. Injustice; inequity	22	3	24	17
3. Community welfare	7	21	45	53
4. Private interest ascendant	56	46	21	17
Total	100% (27)	100% (28)	100% (29)	100% (30)
German				
1. Compliance: direct benefit	—	38	14	3
2. Injustice; inequity	—	24	31	31
3. Community welfare	—	17	41	55
4. Private interest ascendant	—	21	14	10
Total		100% (29)	100% (29)	100% (29)

America: $X^2 = 47.39$ (9), $p < .001$; England: $X^2 = 27.63$ (9), $p < .01$; Germany[a]: $X^2 = 16.90$ (6), $p < .01$

a. Chi-square restrictions are not met; therefore, the chi square is considerably inflated. (The expected frequency in more than 20% of the cells is less than 5.)

"sense of community." Regardless of nationality, the adolescents in our sample develop, by the age of eighteen, a perspective which allows them to judge public policy by viewing it from the standpoint of public interest. At the beginning of adolescence, we see a narrower frame of reference employed: the youngster is more often attuned to the direct benefits to particular individuals of a proposed policy. On occasion, the younger subject does seem to adduce the public interest in that he will favor laws which require the individual to submit to collective authority, but when he does so, he is generally unable to articulate an underlying conception of the public interest and argues rather that "laws should be obeyed."

What is equally striking in the developmental findings is the increasing capacity to balance private and public interests in the process of achieving a judgment. The older adolescent does not exalt the public good at the cost of the private will: to the contrary, there is a heightened sensitivity to the legitimacy of special interests, whether they be those of the individual or of a subgroup within the society. While the state may have the right to insist, ultimately, on the hegemony of the public welfare and safety, it must strive not to infringe upon the rights of the individual citizen. Indeed, the concept of rights and the idea of the public good seem to develop concurrently, and in their interaction produce that denser texture of reasoning that distinguishes late- from early-adolescent political thought.

Another way of characterizing this development is to say that the older adolescent has a more differentiated view of the individual's relationship to the community. He does not separate so sharply the interests of the citizen from those of the polity, and can perceive that the person may benefit as the larger social group in which he lives advances. He can also appreciate the fact that any given individual has multiple reference groups, e.g., the community as a whole as well as his particular occupational group or religious denomination.

This more complex manner of arriving at political judgments does not seem to be general until the age of fifteen, and it may seem puzzling that political thought seems to mature at a somewhat slower pace than moral reasoning. Piaget and his colleagues (Inhelder and Piaget, 1958) have shown that the capacity for formal operations is well established by the age of thirteen. Furthermore, ideas of contract are visible in the moral domain by the age of thirteen; at this age adolescents view moral rules as devices for regulating human relationships. If the participants agree to change the rules they can, providing the participants agree. In corresponding situations in the political domain, rules possess a sacred quality for a somewhat longer period of time; the thirteen-year-old is more likely to see political rules, or laws, as inviolate.

In all likelihood, this apparent lag in political thinking is a function of the child's narrower social perspective. There is some evidence in our interviews that younger adolescents do indeed utilize more advanced moral principles in political reasoning, but are limited to applying them to the face-to-face social situation. The more remote political domain is unfamiliar and in some ways unreal, and thus does not engage those cognitive capacities available in more familiar contexts. Inhelder and Piaget (1958: 348-349) have arrived at a similar conclusion.

> The notions of humanity, social justice (in contrast to interindividual justice which is deeply experienced at the concrete level),

freedom of conscience, civic or intellectual courage, and so forth, like the idea of nationality, are ideas which profoundly influence the adolescent's affective life; but with the child's mentality, except for certain individual glimpses, they can be neither understood nor felt.

In other words, the child does not experience as social feelings anything more than interindividual affects. Even moral sentiments are felt only as a function of unilateral respect (authority) or mutual respect. But *beginning at 13-15 years* feelings about *ideals* or *ideas* are added to the earlier ones.

Cross-National Findings

The differences among the national samples are fairly clear for the most part. The sense of community—that is, the tendency to formulate political problems in terms of the public interest—is strongly developed among the American subjects. Indeed, for every question for which community welfare or public good was a relevant coding the American sample scored highest in this category. At the same time, American adolescents were more likely to be advocates of negative freedom. Keeping both these trends in mind, their overall orientation might best be described as equalitarian. The terms of the implicit social contract run along these lines: The citizen should orient himself voluntarily to the common good, yet he is allowed to depart from collective goals—either as an individual or as a member of a smaller collectivity—just so long as his so doing does not endanger the public welfare. The American subject rarely loses sight of the community.

The British do not present quite so clear a picture as the Americans do; indeed, in order to understand them more fully, we will have to relate the present findings to as-yet-unpublished material (Adelson and Beall, forthcoming) derived from other aspects of the study. What distinguishes the British sample is its adherence, relatively speaking, to the private interest. This tendency displays itself in various ways: sometimes in a kind of bristling individualism, sometimes as a belief in laissez faire, but at all times in a sturdy defense of personal privacy. The individual should be free to pursue his own interests, particularly the economic, without undue interference from the state. Our British subjects did not ordinarily stress the individual's obligation to the community; rather they see the government, ideally, as a disinterested referee, setting down and enforcing the rules of the game. They seem to want the state to protect them against "unfairness," which usually means the greediness or intrusiveness of others. But the great danger of government is that it will transgress its defined role as the impartial referee of private action, and will itself intrude too forcefully into one's affairs.

The German ambiance, too, is only partially visible in these findings. What we do catch a glimpse of is even more strongly evident elsewhere— the emphasis upon rules and obedience. In their interviews a large number of the German adolescents affirm the necessity for accepting the guidance of governmental authority. What these youngsters seem to fear is the disunity of the state; they have in mind a kind of anarchy in which the group is divided and disorganized, and the individual has no clear idea of how to act and what to think. One avoids this dreaded state of inner and outer confusion by submitting to the authority of a benevolent and powerful leader. Perhaps it should be stressed that their attitude towards deviance and dissent is not primarily a punitive one. Rather it seems to be a matter of bringing the wandering sheep back into the fold. Hence the emphasis (on the vaccination item) of persuading the dissident religious sect to change their minds. To put it another way, in many of the German interviews we find a docile, dependent, almost childlike attitude towards government authority. Our interviews appear to support that viewpoint which sees the German propensity for authoritarian government as an outcome, in part, of an overprotective family milieu, which breeds dependency and an overly strong need for approval (Rodnick, 1948).

The degree to which we can generalize these findings to the respective national populations is, of course, unknown; the usual cautions are in order. None of the national tendencies we have discussed is discordant with other observations, impressionistic or systematic, of the countries studied. There are, for example, clear consonances between our findings and those of Almond and Verba (1963).

More to the point, perhaps, is that by and large developmental similarities are stronger than national differences. The acquisition of political concepts in adolescence seems to follow roughly the same path in the three nations, governed, we may conjecture, by the processes of cognitive maturation common to the period. National nuances and variations make themselves felt within the larger framework provided by cognitive growth.

REFERENCES

ADELSON, J., B. GREEN and R. O'NEIL (1969) "The growth of the idea of law in adolescence." Developmental Psychology, 1: 27-32.

ADELSON, J. and R. O'NEIL (1966) "The growth of political ideas in adolescence: the sense of community." J. of Personality and Social Psychology, 4: 295-306.

ALMOND, G. and S. VERBA (1963) The Civic Culture. Princeton: Princeton Univ. Press.

BARRY, B. (1965) Political Argument. New York: Humanities Press.

GREENSTEIN, F. I. (1965) Children and Politics. New Haven and London: Yale Univ. Press.

HESS, R. and J. TORNEY (1967) The Development of Political Attitudes in Children. Chicago: Aldine.

INHELDER, B. and J. PIAGET (1958) The Growth of Logical Thinking from Childhood to Adolescence. New York: Basic Books.

RODNICK, D. (1948) Postwar Germans. New Haven: Yale Univ. Press.

PREADULT DEVELOPMENT OF POLITICAL PARTY IDENTIFICATION IN WESTERN DEMOCRACIES

JACK DENNIS and DONALD J. McCRONE

JACK DENNIS *is Associate Professor of Political Science at the University of Wisconsin, Madison. He is coauthor of* Children in the Political System *and has written articles on political socialization and on mass political behavior.* DONALD J. McCRONE *is Assistant Professor of Political Science at the University of Wisconsin, Madison, and Visiting Senior Lecturer in Government, University of Essex, Colchester, England. He has published, among others, a number of articles treating causal models.*

Students of politics have long been intrigued by the question of the legitimacy of major institutions of government. Only in the decade of the sixties, however, has this fascination been translated into intensive empirical research. A principal approach that has emerged is to gauge the orientations of the mass public toward these institutions. Investigators in America have recently given detailed attention to the extent of confidence the general populace has in legislative bodies (Boynton et al., 1968; Patterson et al., 1969), the judiciary (Dolbeare, 1967; Murphy and Tanenhaus, 1968), political parties (Dennis, 1966), and elections (Dennis, 1970). Other inquiries, less specifically focused upon particular political institutions, have also expanded our knowledge in this connection: for example, the five-nation study of political culture (Almond and Verba, 1963), and some of the leading electoral studies (Campbell et al., 1960, 1966; Butler and Stokes, 1969).

As one key part of this general thrust of behavioral and related research, the political parties have come under special scrutiny as an object of legitimation in democratic regimes. In the voting studies, for example, parties have been considered both at the level of behavioral legitimation—in evidence on the relative proportion of the eligible population that turns out on election day to support one or another party's candidates and programs—and at the level of orientation and commitment—in the data on extent of enduring self-identification with a given party that electors maintain over time.

The latter aspect of legitimation of political parties is the special focus of the present paper. Broadly conceived, our concern is with political party identification as an indicator of diffuse support for the system of parties. In these terms, what the Michigan Survey Research Center studies have shown, inter alia, is that Americans have quite high support for the partisan institution (see Greenstein 1963: 32; Robinson et al., 1968: 496). Few voters in the United States keep themselves completely apart from the major parties; and the very extensive set of partisan feelings serve to structure mass interpretation of the issues of public policy, the meaning of political events, evaluations of candidates, and consequently the outcome of elections. Such pervasive partisan identification implicitly indicates a state of high legitimation.

This is true even though many members of the general public, when queried directly about how well the party system performs or how fully the partisan principle ought to be applied in political life, express serious reservations—and indeed a degree of anti-party sentiment (Dennis, 1966). Americans nevertheless make wide and steady use of the party system through the personal mechanism of partisan self-affiliation in spite of a sense that the parties are deficient in important aspects.

To say, however, that Americans broadly support the party system fails to elicit the dynamics of this support, whatever utility such a statement may have as static description. (Description of this system does provide a benchmark of comparison with other similar systems in the same period, for example.) We must still ask, What are the factors contributing to rising or falling levels of mass commitment to the partisan institution, factors that contribute to its preservation or decline?

An obvious direction in which to move for an answer is to an examination of life cycle and generational experiences, and particularly to preadult learning of partisan orientations. One asks what pattern of evolution of partisan self-images pertains to the sector of the life cycle from early childhood to maturity. Do partisan loyalties become fixed before adolescence, for example, and thus are they crystallized before partisan information supporting partisan choices is likely to have been attained in more than rudimentary form? To chart the preadult sequence of aggregate partisan development is a first important step in probing the dynamics of party-system support. We shall presently want to take this step.

A second significant extension of empirical inquiry from simple description of American adult levels of partisan affiliation is to give the analysis cross-cultural perspective. In the present investigation we attempt such a strategy. We undertake to provide an initial cross-national analysis of preadult patterns of partisan socialization in a number of major Western democracies. Our basic questions will be: (1) When do partisan identifications typically arise in these countries, and what do the shapes of the various learning curves suggest about changing levels of support for the institution of parties? (2) To what extent is the child's attainment of party identification a function of parental transmission to the younger generation? We utilize for this analysis original survey data collected in 1966-1969 in Britain, France, West Germany, Italy, Belgium, and Holland. Our evidence has been derived from interviews and questionnaires administered to children, their parents, and to national samples of adults in the six countries.[1] We will also compare these data from Europe with some existing evidence on the growth of partisan feeling among American youth.

Operational Perspective

Although we approach the subject of party identification from a rather uncommon research perspective, using recent original data on preadult political socialization in a cross-national context, we are nevertheless fortunate in being able to build in a cumulative way upon an existing body of theory and evidence related directly to the aims of the present research. A most pertinent precursor of our concerns is the widely known study by Converse and Dupeux (1962). Using adult data collected in France and the United States roughly a decade before our own study, they set forth a series of suggestive hypotheses which we are able to apply in a replicative vein to our data.

In essence, what they proposed of relevance for our study was that the stability of the party system depends upon high levels of aggregate party identification and that collective levels of partisan affiliation are a function of political socialization. They observed that 75% of Americans, but only 45% of Frenchmen, were able to locate themselves as psychological members of their country's parties (Converse and Dupeux, 1962: 9).

The limited party attachment in France and high attachment in America appeared to be linked to the degree to which parental party identification was communicated to each new generation. They found that 82% of Americans, but only 28% of French respondents, could give an account of their father's partisan orientation. This very large discontinuity apparent in parental transmission in France is attributed to the French parent's tendency to be uncommunicative about his political behavior before his children, an inference supported by implication in other research (see the references in MacRae, 1967: 330-335).

From these observations they drew the system-level inference that the stability of the party system is profoundly affected by political socialization processes. In the French case, partisan socialization results in an electorate heavily populated by voters feeling no continuing party attachments: on the American side, socialization provides an electorate collectively high in commitment to partisan self-images (Converse and Dupeux, 1962: 12-15).

Illuminating as is this analysis for our purposes, several important elements nonetheless need to be added. One addition that we make is a simple but marked methodological departure in the kind of evidence to be used. Converse and Dupeux had available to them only retrospective reports by adult offspring of their parents' partisan orientations. As is now widely recognized, reports by adults of their parents' behavior while these adults were children are susceptible to the disabilities of failing memory, to the psychic need of some children to appear consonant with parental preferences, or to confusion resulting from instability of the parents' preference during the period that his child was maturing (see, for example, Niemi, 1967). An obvious advance in method is thus to measure the preference of parent and child independently during the time that the offspring is still a child. A special benefit of this procedure, where children of different ages are queried, is that child and parent correspondence levels can be computed for different ages of the child.[2] Our present data, for all of their other limitations, do allow us this more satisfactory procedure for estimating varying parental influence on partisanship; and we are fortunate in being able to make these estimates cross-nationally. Indeed, our available data set includes in its variety of countries the two covered by the Converse-Dupeux inquiry. By a different type of evidence, therefore, we are able to extend a key part of their analysis.

Another substantively important addition to the theoretical discussion that we would want to make is to pay attention not only to the aggregate level of partisan orientations, but also to the role of intensity of preference.[3] In a more recent article by Converse (1969), this aspect of the problem is treated in a quite penetrating way and in a manner that provides clear direction for fuller comparative analysis of the relation between preadult socialization and party system stabilization. What we would do to provide a fuller theoretical basis for our analysis is in a sense to put the earlier Converse-Dupeux and the later Converse analyses together.

The argument that emerges when the two works are taken jointly is simply that the party system will be affected both by the level or aggregate extent of partisan feeling and by how intense (and thus aggregatively durable) partisanship has become—a thesis which one of the present authors had at an earlier point argued for as well (McCrone, 1966). Thus on the one hand, aggregate intensity of partisan self-images and collective extent of preference will in theory affect the parties' capacity to function. On the other hand, extent and intensity are both undoubtedly linked to earlier socializing experiences. By means of these two aspects of partisan preference the party system's fate is linked to the character of a country's socialization of its young.

To summarize our operational perspective, therefore, we present the following series of interlinked hypotheses:

(1) Party system stability, in the sense of a persisting configuration of organized partisan competition, is a function of how widely rooted in mass public consciousness is the sense of identification with the parties. Two aspects of mass identification are important: (a) the extent of partisan identification as measured by the proportion of the general public who identify themselves psychologically with one or another of the parties, however intensely; (b) the intensity of party affiliation, seen as the percent of identifiers who have a strong (and thus, more enduring) sense of commitment to one of the parties.

(2) A major factor affecting extent of party identification is cross-generational, intrafamilial transmission of partisan self-images during the progeny's preadult years. An operational measure appropriate in this case is the proportion of all children at a given age who mirror their parents' preferences, i.e., the degree of parent-child correspondence.

(3) Aggregate intensity of partisanship is likely to be a special function of the average duration of individual party identification. Earlier work on electoral behavior has demonstrated the cumulative effects of holding and acting upon partisan preferences over an extended period of time (Campbell et al., 1960). We would extend this hypothesis to preadult socialization by noting that the earlier in life the typical member of the system attains a partisan self-image, the more intense (and durable) such a self-image becomes. This occurs for several possible reasons. One is simply that intensive partisanship is due to the increased opportunities for reinforcing displays of self-partisanship as time passes, other things being equal. Even more significant is the fact that the child is especially impressionable in his formative years so far as basic self-definitions are concerned. As has been noted in the psychological literature,

the seeds of adult behavior take firmest root when they are planted during the primary years of development. For the aggregate of individuals, therefore, the earlier the average person identifies with a party, the greater will be the level of intense collective partisan feeling.

(4) Party system stability is therefore a function of: (a) the extent of family transmission of party identification; and (b) how early the typical member learns to identify himself with a party.

We have not attempted to test every one of these hypotheses in the present investigation. Our enterprise is considerably more modest in scope. We offer a preliminary discussion of some of the major variables on the socialization side of this simple model; and we try, within the limits of our available data, to extend some of the remarks by Converse and his associates. Our central foci will be upon describing the patterns of emergence of preadult party identification and upon the degree of parental transmission in selected western countries. Our main contribution will be greater empirical specification of the model by giving more direct, timely, and comparative evidence necessary for estimating the model's socialization parameters. In addition, we will try to offer some insights into possible implication of our data for other primary variables of the model, such as party system stability.

A caveat to be emphasized from the outset is that, even were we able to make less limited estimates than our present data permit, we would not regard the simple model described above as perfectly self-contained. Exogenous variables such as the relative age of the party system in each country, the relative constancy of party organizations, leaders, and symbols, and the varying activities of elites in restructuring the institutional context of partisan competition, among others, may dampen or enhance aggregate partisan feeling quite apart from socialization. We are thus conscious of dealing only with a portion of partisan reality in these systems by means of this approach.

Not only exogenous, but also reciprocal, causation is to be expected. The relative fixity of the major components of the party system may have socializing effects as, for example, in how well provided are constant partisan targets of citizen apperception during youthful development. If the objects are transitory and ill defined, then as people mature partisanship should emerge less rapidly and distinctly than in stable systems.

A third major qualification is that we would expect future research to find that the effects of early identification and parental influence are less exclusive than we have set them out above with regard to extent or intensity of preference. At an aggregate level, for example, extent and intensity are certainly not fully independent—as shown in Figure 1. Indeed, there is possibly a curvilinear, J-shaped function existing between them for a number of countries for which data are readily available.

When aggregate intensity (percent of those having a partisan identification who respond that they have a strong partisan preference) is plotted against extent of preference (percent who identify to any degree with the parties), we find, even with roughly comparable measures, some pattern of association over seven nations. In the United States, Uruguay, and Great Britain, where identification with parties was highest in this period, over 70% were identified, and of these, more than two thirds were strong identifiers. By contrast, Italy and Mexico have less than half identified, and among party supporters, less than half are committed identifiers. The intermediate cases are Norway and the German Federal Republic, where extent is higher than in Italy and Mexico but intensity is slightly less.

That aggregate intensity and extent of partisan preference are related suggests that socialization factors contributing to increases in the one may serve to augment the other. The relationships briefly set out in our model above are not, therefore, exclusive ones. Family transmission could well affect both intensity and extent of preference; and early learning, *pari passu*, has implications for both aspects of identification. We would call for an expansion of the terms of the model, therefore, in future work. With these considerations in mind, let us turn to our socialization data.

PREADULT GROWTH OF PARTISAN IDENTIFICATION

The most widely accepted descriptive hypothesis about the time of origin of party identification during the life cycle of the average American (as derived both from studies of voting and of political socialization) is that partisan self-images typically take root before voting age, beginning for many as early as the first years of school. Greenstein (1965: 71) observed for example: "By fourth grade more than six out of ten of the New Haven children were able to state whether their party preference was Republican or Democratic: this although little more than a third of the fourth graders could name even one public representative from either of the two major parties and less than a fifth could name a leader of each of the parties." Easton and Hess (1962: 245) in another early study formed a

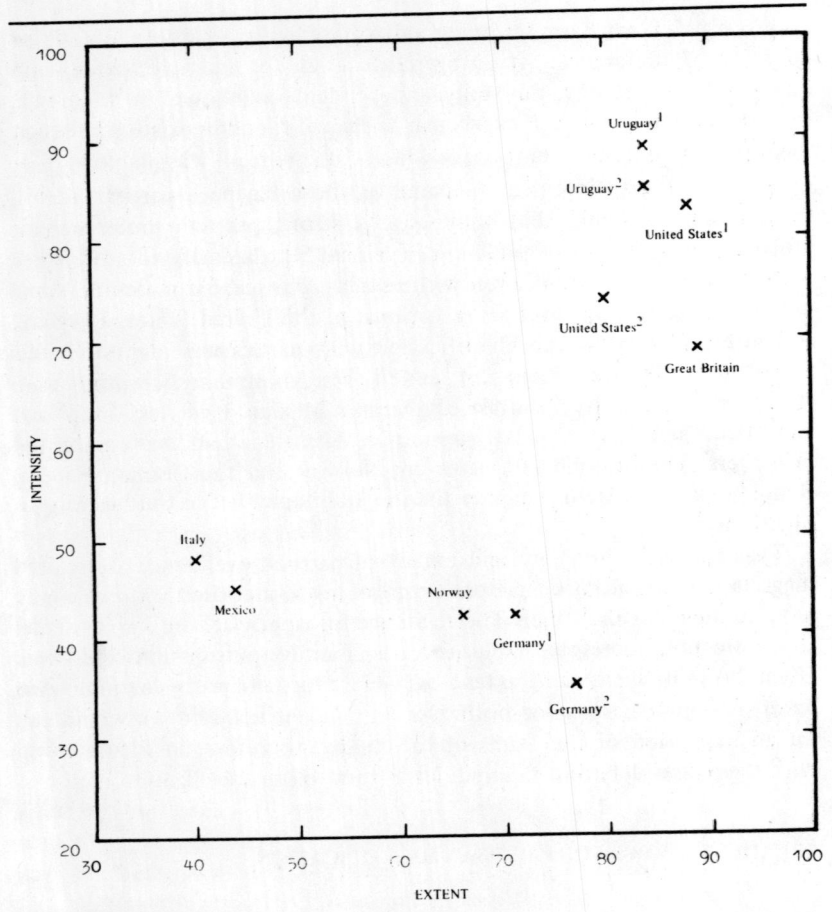

[122] COMPARATIVE POLITICAL SOCIALIZATION

Data Sources:
(1) For Italy, Mexico, Great Britain, Germany[1], and United States[2]: Almond-Verba Five-Nation Study.
(2) Norway: Valen and Katz, 1964.
(3) Germany[2]: Zohlnhöfer, 1965.
(4) United States: Robinson et al., 1968.
(5) Uruguay: Original data supplied by Donald McCrone. Two samples were used, one in Montevideo and the other in the interior (outside Montevideo).

Figure 1. RELATION OF INTENSITY TO EXTENT OF PARTY IDENTIFICATION, BY NATION

similar conclusion: "In a pre-test sample of about 700 children, a strong majority in each grade from two through eight state that if they could vote they would align themselves with either of the two major parties in the United States."[4]

A question one may raise about these results is whether such wide early identification is replicated in the learning curves of other nations. Let us consider the data in Table 1 to evolve a preliminary answer.

In this table we present the evidence from two sets of cross-national surveys of youth. The first survey was conducted in three European countries in 1966-1967 and the other in six European nations in 1969. Earlier American data from national studies of preadult political socialization are also included as bases of comparison for the European data.

We note first a fairly general pattern of heightened party identification with increasing age in the four countries for which we have preadolescent data. In the pre-1969 data, party identification increases in the United States, Germany, and Italy, and remains roughly the same in Britain. In the 1969 data, however—and these data cover a later portion of the age span—these trends are not fully sustained. There is an apparent tendency toward late-adolescent leveling off of partisanship.

The major exception to the pattern of progressive preadolescent-to-adolescent rise in partisan identification is Britain where, even by the ages of eight through ten, four out of five children have come to identify themselves as partisans. The British pattern stands out both because of the early-attained high level of collective identification and by the continuation of this high partisanship with slight variation into adulthood. There is much merit in the Gilbert and Sullivan hypothesis that every child in England who is born alive is either a little Liberal or Conservative—if we adjust for the subsequent addition of the Labour Party and for a modest level of nonidentification.

We are supported in our conclusion about this British pattern by other findings. Abramson's and Inglehart's (1970: n. 36) separately obtained samples of English secondary-school students each demonstrated that well over eighty percent identified with one of the three major parties. This remarkably high level of early partisanship contrasts with the more gradual patterns observed for America, Germany, and Italy. Such broadly based preferences, established when the child is still relatively young in Britain, give and most likely will continue to give the British party system its special character of high citizen identification and legitimation. The ability of the party system to continue to penetrate deeply the electoral and governmental processes of decision-making in the future is founded upon what appears to be an extensive base of partisan self-identification. Such identification has already flowered among the upcoming generation of Britons. The less complete Belgian and Dutch data suggest that a similar pattern pertains for these systems.

TABLE 1
PREADULT PARTY IDENTIFICATION, BY AGE AND NATION

		AGE			
		Youngest	Younger Middle	Older Middle	Oldest
NATION					
United States	1960-1961	49[a] (1749)[b]	56[a] (1723)	—	—
	1965	—	—	64[c] (1852)	—
Great Britain	1966-1967	80 (140)	79 (205)	79 (190)	—
	1969	—	—	87 (47)	82 (78)
West Germany	1966	50 (144)	62 (219)	68 (135)	—
	1969	—	—	83 (46)	79 (51)
Italy	1966	45 (117)	51 (115)	55 (116)	—
	1969	—	—	65 (68)	64 (69)
France	1969	—	—	61 (54)	61 (44)
Netherlands	1969	—	—	80 (35)	83 (35)
Belgium	1969	—	—	76 (38)	78 (37)
AGE GROUPINGS					
United States	1960-1961	9-10	12-13	—	—
	1965	—	—	17-18	—
Great Britain	1966-1967	8-10	11-13	14-17	—
	1969	—	—	15-17	18-21
Germany	1966	9-10	11-13	14-16	—
	1969	—	—	15-16	19-20
Italy	1966	10	13	16	—
	1969	—	—	15-16	19-20
France	1969	—	—	15-16	19-20
Netherlands	1969	—	—	15-16	19-20
Belgium	1969	—	—	15-16	19-20

a. Data from Eight City Study, 1961-1962 (see Easton and Dennis, 1969, for study description).
b. Numbers in parentheses are used as the base for percentage.
c. Data from the SRC H.S. Seniors Study (see Jennings and Niemi, 1968a).

Italy and France, by contrast, are nearer the other end of the continuum in extent of early identification; and France, bearing in mind the fragmentary character of our French data, is apparently the lowest of all. Such conclusions about France and Italy fit our expectations as derived from earlier sources. Converse and Dupeux (1962) had noted the disparity between France and the United States; and we do find a difference in the predicted direction, although it is not of the magnitude we would have thought likely from the earlier data. Again, Converse (1969), drawing upon the Almond-Verba data, had elicited similar comparisons for Italy—showing on partisan intensity that Italy is lowest and Britain highest.

In France, Roig and Billon-Grand (1968) have more recently demonstrated how little identified French children are with the parties. This is a finding that complements the earlier Converse-Dupeux evidence from the perspective of preadult socialization.[5] Greenstein and Tarrow (1969) observe, in their interpretative review of Roig and Billon-Grand: "The Grenoble study, then, appears to corroborate the Converse and Dupeux finding that the great bulk of French children fail to acquire party identification." Our own evidence certainly does confirm the lower level of French preadult party identification.

A qualification that we would emphasize, however, is that our recent data do not conform fully to earlier evidence when we consider the level of youthful party identification in France. There is a substantial majority in our data who are identified. The earlier hypothesis was that there is extreme failure to form partisan identifications before adulthood in France. This is not confirmed by our recent observations—which suggests a possible trend. We will return to this point.

Italy's position, nearer to France than to Britain or Germany, is certainly in line with whatever projections one is apt to make from the Almond-Verba data. To show this graphically we fit in a speculative way our "Cross-National Study of Political Socialization" (C.N.S.P.S.) data to the Almond-Verba Five-Nation Study (A-V) data, in Figure 2.

However great may have been the disparities in time of data collection, types of surveys, and question wording, our evidence does conform remarkably to what we would have expected from the five-nation study about the relative positions of youthful aggregate, partisan orientation across countries. The British, having begun very early on a high plane of identification continue, after a temporary drop between adolescence and voting age, as the highest of all four nations in extent of partisanship right

[126] COMPARATIVE POLITICAL SOCIALIZATION

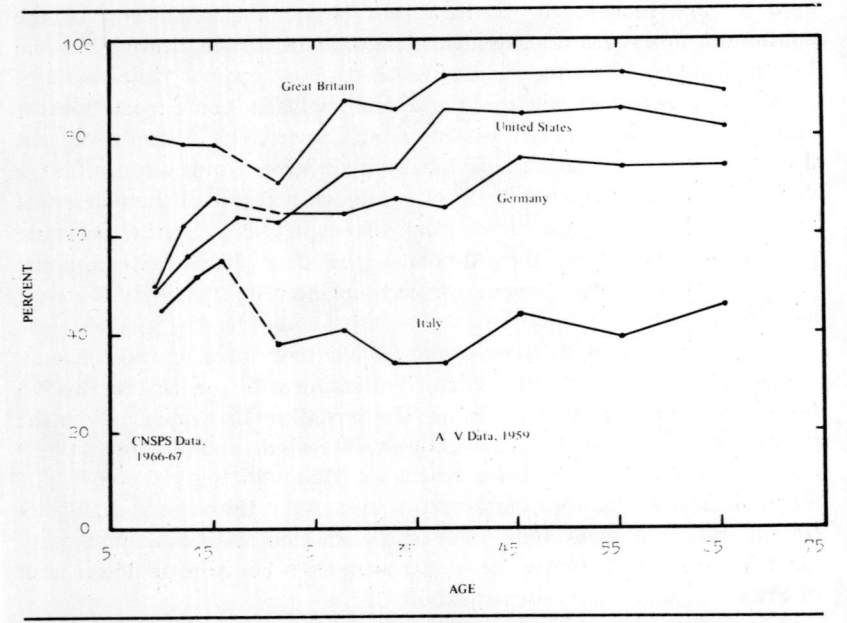

Figure 2. EXTENT OF PARTY IDENTIFICATION IN GERMANY, GREAT BRITAIN, ITALY, AND UNITED STATES, BY AGE

across the age span. There is a modest accretion of adult party identification after voting age; but this gain is relatively small in comparison to the increase prior to age eight.

The United States on this projection shows a similar, if lower, adult level of identification to that of Britain; but there is a more gradual age progression of preference from childhood to middle age. The more striking contrast to the British is the extent of partisanship among Italians, both young and old. The Italians are only about half as identified with the parties as are the British.

When children and adults in Italy are compared with each other, however, one detects a higher level of partisanship among the youth than for the grownups. Either the partisan experience of adulthood has a depressant effect upon youthful identification, or else our later youth data may reflect some generational partisan shift in Italy. The 1969 data support the finding of a higher than expected level of youthful Italian partisan orientation (see Table 1). While Italians may be generally lower in the extent of collective cathexis with the party system than is true in the other countries, except France, we may be observing a secular trend toward the levels enjoyed by the more stable party systems—if our rough data give us indications of the future. The French, as noted earlier, may be experiencing a similar upward trend.[6]

Germany is perhaps the most interesting of all in that a more "severe" pattern of early learning of partisanship is observed than for Americans; but the corresponding level of adult partisanship is not apparent. One suspects, as for Italy, some generational trend in which newer members of the system are being more readily assimilated to the partisan system even though they may not fully approve of partisan competition and the present operation of the parties (Dennis et al., 1968). Other data have shown Germans to exhibit partisan intensity and extent of identification at levels comparable to those of the Americans. This was true even a decade ago (Zohlnhöfer, 1965), and it reinforces our general conclusions. Germans would appear to be changing gradually the degree of popular legitimacy of partisan institutions; and their partisanship could soon surpass that of Americans and equal that of the British.

We might briefly pursue the latter hypothesis by viewing the 1969 German and British data in conjunction with the earlier Five-Nation and C.N.S.P.S. evidence. This set of comparisons is presented in graphical form in Figure 3.

By plotting extent of party identification by age for earlier and later points in the United Kingdom and West Germany, we find that the younger half portion of the German 1969 curve of party identification is clearly above the line defined by earlier observations, while the British are if anything slightly lower than in the previous period. In both instances, the British respondents show higher levels of identification; but the 1969 European Youth Survey (E.Y.S.) curves depict a narrowing of the difference. Obviously, given the limitations of the data, we cannot push this inference very far. Yet we cannot overlook the fact that the Germans, both from our own and other evidence (see Zohlnhöfer) seem to be becoming increasingly partisan; the change is one that augurs greater stabilization of the type experienced previously by the British, the Scandinavians, and few others.

This movement of German partisanship certainly represents a more thoroughgoing system change since World War II than is true for Italy. Both nations have had a period of continuous partisan competition during that time, but the institutional progression on this indicator has been more extensive in the case of Germany. Mass legitimation of the parties on the level of personal identification, especially for youth, has begun to approach in the Federal Republic the standard of the most settled western democracies.

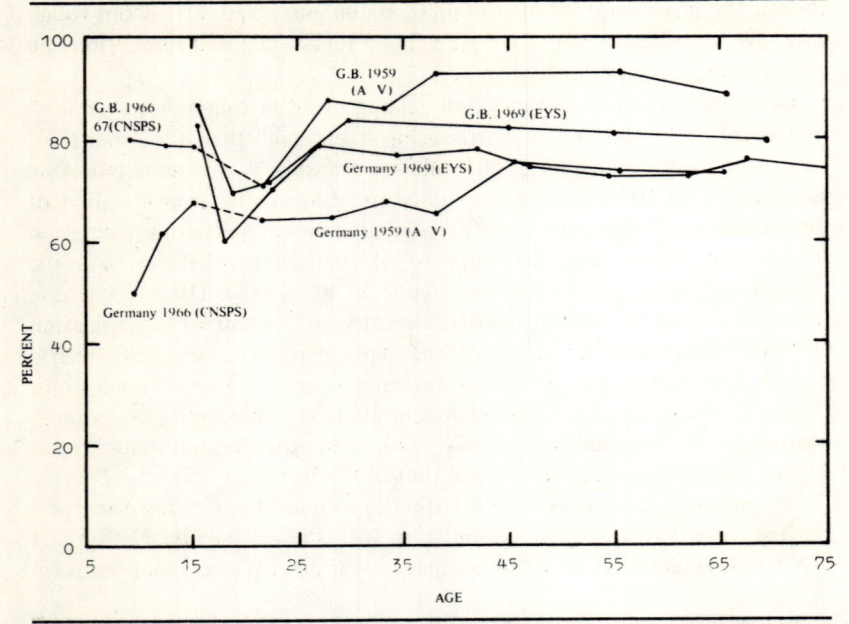

Figure 3. EXTENT OF POLITICAL PARTY IDENTIFICATION IN BRITAIN AND GERMANY, 1959 AND 1969, BY AGE

Before we conclude our discussion of national differences in youthful partisan development let us consider one further issue, namely, the degree to which parents in these various countries influence the partisan choices of their children.

CHILD-PARENT CORRESPONDENCE IN PARTY IDENTIFICATION

What past research in America has shown is that children resemble their parents in partisan choice to a marked extent. Substantial parent-child correlation has been demonstrated both in the voting studies which use adult offsprings' retrospective reports of their parents' preferences (see Berelson et al., 1954: 89; Campbell et al., 1960: 147), and in political socialization studies, where children and their parents have been interviewed separately (see Hyman, 1959: 70-72; Jennings and Niemi, 1968a: 172-174).

In turning to other nations, we might well expect significant departures from this American pattern of high association: Converse and Dupeux (1962) showed a considerably lower rate of awareness by the French child

TABLE 2
PARENT-CHILD AGREEMENT IN PARTY IDENTIFICATION BY AGE AND NATION

		AGE			
		Youngest	Younger Middle	Older Middle	Oldest
NATIONS					
United States	1965	—	—	59%[a] (1852)	—
Great Britain	1969	—	—	36 (47)	42 (78)
West Germany	1966	47% (144)	49 (218)	57 (135)	—
	1969	—	—	41 (44)	50 (30)
France	1969	—	—	29 (44)	19 (54)
AGE GROUPINGS					
United States	1965	—	—	17-18	—
Great Britain	1969	—	—	15-17	18-21
Germany	1966	9-10	11-13	14-16	—
	1969	—	—	15-16	19-20
France	1969	—	—	15-16	19-20

a. Recalculated from the Jennings-Niemi data cited in Table 1.

of his parents' political perspectives. Our hypothesis would be that the less stable party systems such as France would show little parent-child correspondence, whereas the stable European party systems should approach the American levels. What do we find?

Table 2 presents data which give greater cross-national perspective than has been possible heretofore, though these data are even less complete than our evidence on age-related development.

Relative to the hypotheses of Converse and Dupeux (1962), we do observe a noteworthy difference between French and American rates of correspondence across generations. French children's resemblance to the partisan orientation of their parents is less than half that for the Americans if we use the Jennings-Niemi data as our base of comparison. Not only do the French pass on their partisan preferences to their offspring at a low rate, but this rate actually declines as the child gets older—suggesting low familial reinforcement for whatever partisan cues are transmitted. The

German and British parents, by contrast, show increasing partisan similarity with their children as the latter move through adolescence.[7]

One possible effect of these different patterns will be to maintain the party systems differentially. The French party is likely to sustain part of its past volatility of partisan organization in the future. This would work in a direction contrary to whatever may have been the impetus from Gaullism. Gaullism has attempted to defactionalize and stabilize party options in recent years, but socialization's net effects are in the opposite direction.

Looking at the other systems, we might expect on these grounds that the American parties should be able to resist change as before.[8] At the same time, we should note the potential lessons from our earlier analysis when we turn to Britain. While the familial carryover of partisan self-images is lower for the British than for the Americans, one should bear in mind the finding presented in Table 1 concerning the early high rate of collective identification in Britain. The latter should receive special emphasis in whatever assessment we make of the British party future.[9]

The Germans fall between the British and Americans in these respects. While having less aggregate preadult partisan identification than the British, the Germans nevertheless show greater generational continuity. On the other hand, compared with Americans, extent of German identification is as high, but parental impact is lower.

For different combinations of reasons, therefore, the British, the Americans, and the Germans are not markedly different in their respective prospects for party system legitimation at this level in the near future. The French, by contrast, are low on both counts, and thereby conform to the Converse-Dupeux propositions. The main qualification one would have to make for France in projecting this outcome is on the grounds of what could be a higher level of youthful identification than in the past. But parent to child reproduction of partisanship in France has continued, as before, to be low.

CONCLUSION

Utilizing recent pilot data from two sets of surveys specifically designed for use in investigating preadult political socialization in six western democracies, we have attempted to add to cumulative knowledge of the growth of partisan identifications. Converse and his associates have provided much of the inspiration for this limited inquiry. Our data are at best fragmentary. Larger numbers of respondents, a better sampling of national systems, and a broader time sequence are obviously needed to give these preliminary notes a more solid empirical foundation.

We have proceeded on the basis of a simple model linking preadult socialization to the stability of party systems. We claim to have shed our provisional illumination only on a few aspects of this model, however. Our main contribution has been to provide additional empirical benchmarks for what we hope will be more sophisticated and more widely grounded specifications of the model in the future.

Once scholarship goes beyond the level of remarking that most people in the major democracies identify with parties and that parents apparently have some role in the partisan education of their children, investigation then demands more precise estimates of the parameters of affiliation as these articulate with the trends in party system legitimation in various national contexts. At this point we need to ask a number of more specific questions. Contemporary scholarship will want to know how many people, with what degrees of intensity and at which points in the political life cycle of the individual, acquire, under what degree of parental influence, partisan self-images. Furthermore, we need to expand the scope of these estimates both across nations and over different partisan epochs within countries. Once we begin to make more precise measurements of these variables, we will then be capable of connecting partisanship as a mode of legitimation to the processes of stabilization or transformation of institutionalized parties. Mass partisanship is important to scholarship not simply as a means of estimating the outcomes of elections, but also as a perspective upon the growth and decay of the party institutions of postindustrial society. Our modest evidence hopefully takes us some distance in understanding the forces behind these institutional phenomena.

The evidence shows a generally consistent pattern of growth of partisan feeling well before voting age in all of these countries. Such development varies in extent by nation. The English child learns very early that he has a partisan choice to make, whereas the French child even in late adolescence is only slightly more apt to be a party identifier than not. Nevertheless, the fact that a majority of French youth do identify is surprising given the results of earlier studies. We may have observed fleetingly the leading edge of a major shift in childhood socialization in France in the sense that rather more new members are being integrated into partisan modes of orientation than was formerly the case.

The Italians would appear to resemble the French in these respects, being both lower than the British in extent of partisanship among youth, but, relative to Italian adults, perhaps moving the aggregate upward. The Germans by contrast are particularly noteworthy in their closer rivalry to British and American levels of early partisanship. The Germans also show a possible generational trend in favor of the parties. The young German, more like the young Britisher than the Italian, is rather likely to become an early partisan. Comparison of earlier and later German data reinforces this image of aggregate partisan increase in the past decade in Germany. From this point of view the Germans have had the most far-reaching alteration of partisan patterns of any of the three large continental-European democracies in the direction of resembling the older party systems of America and Britain. But all three continental nations show some signs of youthful change.

On parent-to-child transmission, a relatively consistent pattern with the above is observed: the French, as expected, are low; the U.S. is high; and the Germans and British are in between. French parents to a low degree reproduce their political preferences in their children, and such partisan images as are reproduced early are not as likely to be parentally reinforced as the child grows older. In Britain and Germany, by contrast, wider influence of parents is indicated and this influence becomes extended as children get older.

Limited and preliminary as our inquiry has been, we do see some gross contours of future partisan change in these systems. Our expectation would be that America and Britain would continue to show a high engagement of their citizens in the partisan aspects of the system. The West Germans appear to be overtaking the Anglo-American systems in the extent of mass interiorization of partisan feeling.

Belgians and the Dutch show high early partisanship as well; thus they indicate a future not unlike the British or German systems. France and Italy denote some lesser degree of mass consciousness of self-partisanship. We would thus expect the partisan volatility of the past to continue. Yet we observe also a possible indication of higher levels of youthful partisan awareness than in the past in these two nations. The susceptibility for destabilization may be waning, and a slower, but perceptible trend of partisan institutionalization could be occurring. This is a question that we will have to leave for future analysis.

NOTES

1. We are indebted to a number of people for cooperation in gathering these data. The first series of surveys were carried out in England, Germany, and Italy, in 1966-1967. We were fortunate to have the help in England of Professors Anthony

King and Jean Blondel of the University of Essex; Judith Goldman; and Humphrey Taylor of the Opinion Research Centre. In Italy we were aided by Professor Pierpaolo Luzzatto Fegiz of DOXA. Our German data in this series were collected by Klaus Liepelt and InFAS. The second series of surveys—in Britain, Germany, France, Italy, Holland, and Belgium, in 1969—were carried out through the auspices of INRA with the special cooperation of Jean-Jacques Rabier of the European Common Market, Professor Ronald Inglehart of the University of Michigan, and Professors Leon Lindberg and Stuart Scheingold of the University of Wisconsin.

Our samples are all national in scope with the exception of the British survey of 1966-1967. The latter was drawn from three cities in England: London, Colchester, and Leeds. For the most part, our child and parent samples are based on existing national adult cross-section samples. The exception to the latter is the 1966 Italian Youth Survey, which is an independently drawn national quota sample.

2. One is thus able to trace the extent of reinforcement of preference over the period of preadult maturation. Obvious as are the advantages of such a procedure in terms of a developmental perspective, parent-child comparisons at different ages of the child are still relatively rare in political socialization research. A recent exception is found in Dennis (1969). More generally, the developmental perspective is exemplified, for example, in Easton and Dennis (1969).

3. These authors do allude to intensity as a factor in stabilizing the party system when they note the following: "The durably involved voter tends toward strong partisan commitments and his behavior over time stabilizes party fortunes within a nation " (Converse and Dupeux, 1962: 2).

4. One should also note, however, the concomitant rise in the proportions of elementary-school age American children who come to think of themselves as independents or as having no fixed party preference. A useful brief statement about this effect is found in Jennings and Niemi (1968b: 452-454).

5. What Roig and Billon-Grand (1968: 98-99) seem to indicate are some major causes for the low level of partisan identification among French children is found in the following passage:

> Cette orientation illustre une conséquence de la multiplicité et de l'instabilité des partis: l'engendrement d'ambiguités et de contradictions qui empêchent les individus de formuler leur opinion par référence à un parti. Il ne s'agit pas là d'une caractéristique particulière au processus de socialisation des enfants, mais plutôt d'une caractéristique de la culture et du système politique francais que se manifeste dès l'enfance. Cette lacune est significative et produit ses effets à partir du moment où l'enfant accède à la vie sociale et commence à manifester des orientations et des préférences politiques (douze-treize ans). C'est à ce moment que se trouve bouclé en cercle vicieux que l'on peut schématiser comme suit: une culture politique non partisane entraîne une socialisation politique hors des partis, laquelle engendre une attitude critique ou hostile aux partis; celle-ci crée une culture politique apartisane, etc.

6. One might anticipate some effects of recent youth protest, especially in the universities of these systems. A possible result of these politicizing influences would be to increase the level of political involvement among the broader category of youth and thus its partisanship. Not only in our 1969 French and Italian data, but also in Britain and Germany, do we find what appears to be a higher level of partisanship for

the same age group than was true a few years previously. This could be a difference due simply to sampling variations or alternations in question wording, however. And we must bear in mind that part of these university-sector protests have shown occasionally both antisystem and antiparty sentiment. Thus, some of the carryover of greater politicization to greater partisanship may have been dissipated by the nature of the protest.

7. Whatever scattered evidence there is would appear to support the level of parent-child agreement that we find—at least in Britain. For example, Abrams and Little, using retrospective reports of young adult respondents in a series of N.O.P. surveys in 1964, presented data that, upon recalculation, show a 41% level of agreement of child and parent on party identification (Abrams and Little, 1965: 100; also see Butler and Stokes, 1969: 44-64).

8. It is interesting that even in the 1968 presidential election in America—in which very considerable shifts in candidate preference were observed in comparison with previous elections—the underlying distribution of partisan identification changed very little (Converse et al., 1969). On the other hand, we should bear in mind that the party system may become unhinged at a higher point of mass orientation, for example, in increasingly critical estimations of the worth of the institution of party as a device of government (Dennis, 1966).

9. Butler and Stokes (1969: 52-53) suggest that class milieu may serve as a primary source of partisan cues for those in Britain who begin life without a partisan lead from their parents. Thus, while parental transmission may not be as strong as in other nations, the British are nonetheless more apt to become partisans than is true for the Americans, Japanese, or French, because of the especially strong impetus given by class milieu in Britain.

REFERENCES

ABRAMS, A. and A. LITTLE (1965) "The young voter in British politics." British J. of Sociology 16: 95-109.
ABRAMSON, P. and R. INGLEHART (1970) "The development of systemic support in four western democracies." Comparative Pol. Studies 2 (January): 419-442.
ALMOND, G. and S. VERBA (1963) The Civic Culture. Princeton: Princeton Univ. Press.
BERELSON, B., P. F. LAZARSFELD, and W. McPHEE (1954) Voting. Chicago: Univ. of Chicago Press.
BOYNTON, G. R., S. C. PATTERSON, and R. D. HEDLUND (1968) "The structure of political support for legislative institutions." Midwest J. of Pol. Sci. 12 (May): 163-180.
BUTLER, D. and D. STOKES (1969) Political Change in Britain. New York: St. Martin's.
CAMPBELL, A., P. E. CONVERSE, W. E. MILLER, and D. STOKES (1960) The American Voter. New York: John Wiley.
CONVERSE, P. E. and G. DUPEUX (1969) "Of time and partisan stability." Comparative Pol. Studies 2 (July): 139-171.
——— (1962) "Politicization of the electorate in France and the United States." Public Opinion Q. 26 (Spring): 1-23.

--- W. E. MILLER, J. C. RUSK, and A. C. WOLFE (1969) "Continuity and change in American politics: parties and issues in the 1968 election." Amer. Pol. Sci. Rev. 63 (December): 1083-1105.

DENNIS, J. (1970) "Support for the institution of elections by the mass public." Amer. Pol. Sci. Rev. 64 (September).

--- (1966) "Support for the party system by the mass public." Amer. Pol. Sci. Rev. 60 (September): 600-615.

--- L. LINDBERG, D. McCRONE, and R. STIEFBOLD (1969) "Political socialization to democratic orientations in four western systems." Comparative Pol. Studies 1 (April): 71-101.

--- (1968) Political Learning in Childhood and Adolescence: A Study of Fifth, Eighth and Eleventh Graders in Milwaukee, Wisconsin. Madison: Wisconsin Research and Development Center for Cognitive Learning.

DOLBEARE, K. M. (1967) "The public views the Supreme Court," pp. 194-212 in H. Jacob (ed.) Law, Politics and the Federal Courts. Boston: Little, Brown.

EASTON, D. and R. D. HESS (1962) "The child's political world." Midwest J. of Pol. Sci. 6 (August): 229-246.

--- and J. DENNIS (1969) Children in the Political System: Origins of Political Legitimacy. New York: McGraw-Hill.

GREENSTEIN, F. I. (1965) Children and Politics. New Haven: Yale Univ. Press.

--- (1963) The American Party System and the American People. Englewood Cliffs, N.J.: Prentice-Hall.

--- and S. TARROW (1969) "The study of French political socialization: toward the revocation of paradox." World Politics 22 (October): 95-137.

HYMAN, H. H. (1959) Political Socialization. New York: Free Press.

JENNINGS, M. K. and R. G. NIEMI (1968a) "The transmission of political values from parent to child." Amer. Pol. Sci. Rev. 62 (March): 169-184.

--- (1968b) "Patterns of political learning." Harvard Educational Rev. 38 (Summer): 443-467.

McCRONE, D. J. (1966) "Party identification: a cross-national study." PH.D. dissertation. University of North Carolina.

MacRAE, D. (1967) Parliament, Parties, and Society in France, 1946-1958. New York: St. Martin's.

MURPHY, W. F. and J. TANNENHAUS (1968) "Public opinion and the United States Supreme Court." Law and Society Rev. 2 (May): 357-384.

NIEMI, R. G. (1967) "A methodological study of political socialization in the family." Ph.D. dissertation. University of Michigan.

PATTERSON, S. C., G. R. BOYNTON, and R. D. HEDLUND (1969) "Perceptions and expectations of the legislature and support for it." Amer. J. of Sociology 75 (July): 62-76.

ROBINSON, J. P., J. C. RUSK, and K. B. HEAP (1968) Measures of Political Attitudes. Ann Arbor, Mich.: Institute for Social Research.

ROIG, C. and F. BILLON-GRAND (1968) The Political Socialization of Children. Paris: Armand Colin. [In French]

VALEN, H. and D. KATZ (1964) Political Parties in Norway. London: Tavistock.

ZOHLNHÖFER, W. (1965) "Parteiidentifizierung in der Bundesrepublik und den Vereinigten Staaten." Kölner Zeitschrift für Soziologie und Sozialpsychologie 9: 125-135, 160-166.

DATE DUE

Ap 10 '76			
JAN 20 '77			
MAR 25 '77			
Uc 10 '77			
JAN 15 '78			

DEMCO 38-297